Shane Osborn's
# starters

# Shane Osborn's
# starters

641·812

photographs by David Loftus

## notes

- Ovens and grills must be preheated to the setting specified in the recipe.
- All spoon measures are level unless otherwise stated: 1 tsp = 5 ml spoon; 1 tbsp = 15 ml spoon.
- Use fresh herbs unless dried herbs are suggested.
- Use sea salt and freshly ground black pepper unless otherwise stated.
- Medium eggs should be used except where a different size is specified. Free-range eggs are recommended. Note that a few recipes, including mayonnaise, contain raw or lightly cooked eggs. The young, elderly, pregnant women and anyone with an immune-deficiency disease should avoid these, because of the slight risk of salmonella.

**Publishing director** Jane O'Shea   **Project editor** Janet Illsley   **Art director** Vanessa Courtier   **Photographer** David Loftus
**Food stylist** Shane Osborn   **Production** Beverley Richardson

First published in 2004 by Quadrille Publishing Limited, Alhambra House, 27-31 Charing Cross Road, London WC2H OLS

Cataloguing in Publication Data: a catalogue record for this book is available from the British Library.

ISBN 1 84400 118 0

Printed in China

# Contents

introduction

For me, cooking is about sharing my enjoyment of good food with others. When I say good food, it doesn't have to be gastronomic delights using luxury ingredients, it can be simple food using good fresh produce. Sometimes friends are intimidated when they cook a meal for me, but the one thing all chefs love is to be cooked for. I appreciate all styles of food – seeing and tasting different interpretations of dishes gives me a greater understanding of what customers want to eat.

Although my mother worked as a cook, we never ate extravagantly at home, just simple, tasty food – homemade hamburgers, lasagnes and casseroles, for example – humble dishes made well. My first experience of working in a kitchen was part-time at the age of thirteen, doing all sorts of jobs from peeling vegetables and eggs to washing-up. I began to realise that cooking really excited me and at the age of fifteen I started a four-year chef's apprenticeship in Perth.

The things I remember most about the kitchen were the wonderful smells, colours and textures of the food. School for me was boring and irrelevant, but working in a kitchen was a dream because I was surrounded by food and I loved eating. I remember scoffing handfuls of chocolate from huge bags in the dry stores, always out of the executive chef's view. I was astonished at the wealth of information and foodie stories my senior chefs would relate, most of them originating from France, Britain or Spain. The food in Perth in the late 80's had a French influence, something that gave me a curiosity for France – its culture, language and way of life. In 1991, I decided to come to Europe to see for myself. I was amazed by the fresh produce – salads, herbs, fish and other ingredients that I had never heard of. I came to London thinking I was an experienced chef, but soon realised that there is always something new to learn.

I love experimenting with different ingredients and flavour combinations. 'Starters' was a natural choice for my first cookbook because at the start of a meal appetites are at their keenest and most receptive to new taste experiences. You will find that many of my recipes, especially in the first three chapters, are surprisingly simple, but they do rely on top quality ingredients, so shop well. The recipes in 'Food for groups' are ideal if you are having a party – just increase the quantities to match the number of guests. 'Posh' starters are perfect for smaller gatherings and some – but by no means all – of these are a little more challenging. But don't think of the dishes solely as starters, the recipes are versatile and throughout the book you'll find suggestions for serving them as main courses.

Nothing gives me more pleasure than to see and hear the enjoyment my cooking gives customers and friends. Food is a great catalyst for conversation and it provides lasting memories of travel, people and childhood. It is something that I will always appreciate and I would love everyone to derive as much pleasure from cooking and eating as I do.

# nibbles & snacks

Pickled baby vegetables

Vegetable crisps

Home-roasted nuts with herbs & sea salt

Crisp marinated quail eggs

Curried quail eggs

Button mushroom beignets

Leek & red onion tartlets

Sweet onion & anchovy pastries

Herb-crusted tuna with olive & shallot dressing

Smoked eel pâté with apple & lime

Smoked salmon with horseradish mousse

Pan-fried chicken livers on garlic croûtes

Roasted new potatoes wrapped in Parma ham

Foie gras parfait with poppy seed crisps

# Pickled baby vegetables

SERVES 8–10

**marinade**

*50ml olive oil*

*100g shallots, peeled and
    thinly sliced*

*3 garlic cloves, peeled*

*10g salt*

*5 white peppercorns*

*10 coriander seeds*

*10g thyme sprigs*

*2 bay leaves*

*300ml white wine vinegar*

**vegetables**

*10 baby artichokes*

*20 baby carrots*

*½ small cauliflower florets*

*20 baby onions*

*10 baby aubergines*

*200g girolles or other
    mushrooms*

**marinade**    Heat the olive oil in a medium pan over a low heat. Add the shallots, garlic, salt, peppercorns, coriander seeds, thyme and bay leaves, Stir, then cover and sweat gently, stirring occasionally, for 10–12 minutes until the shallots are soft. Add the wine vinegar and reduce until almost dry, then add 600ml water and bring to the boil. Lower the heat and leave to simmer for 15 minutes.

**preparing the vegetables**    Halve or quarter the artichokes; peel and trim the carrots; cut the cauliflower into tiny sprigs; peel the baby onions; slice the aubergines; trim and clean the mushrooms.

**pickling the vegetables**    Cook each type of vegetable separately. Add to the marinade and simmer gently for 5–10 minutes until just tender; test by piercing with a small sharp knife. Return all the vegetables to the pickling marinade and leave to cool. When cool, the vegetables are ready to serve. (Alternatively, they can be kept chilled in the marinade for up to 1 week.) Strain and reserve the liquid as it can be used to pickle another batch of vegetables; it will keep in the fridge for up to 1 week.

**to serve**    Drain the vegetables and arrange in small bowls or on platters to serve as canapés.

**note**    These pickled baby vegetables have many uses. In the restaurant we serve them as nibbles, garnishes, main course accompaniments and salads – partnered with interesting leaves and herbs. As an accompaniment, pickled cauliflower cuts the richness of salmon and tuna beautifully. In a similar way, the sweet acidity of pickled artichokes is the perfect foil for foie gras and rich terrines.

**as a salad starter** Toss the pickled vegetables with a selection of salad leaves, such as wild rocket, baby chard and young sorrel or spinach. Add wafer-thin slices of smoked duck breast (or Parma ham or bresaola) if you like. Drizzle the salad with a little extra virgin olive oil to serve if required.

# Vegetable crisps

SERVES 10

*2 parsnips*
*1 large sweet potato*
*2 large beetroot*
*3 salsify sticks*
*8 large Jerusalem artichokes*
*oil, to deep-fry*
*sea salt*
*small handful of parsley sprigs*

**preparing the root vegetables**    Peel the vegetables and trim the ends, then cut lengthways into wafer-thin slices, using a mandoline or swivel vegetable peeler.

**deep-frying the crisps**    Heat the oil in a deep-fat fryer or deep, heavy saucepan to 170–180°C. Deep-fry the vegetable slices in small batches (a handful at a time) to ensure they cook evenly. Add to the hot oil and deep-fry for 15–30 seconds until they just start to crisp and colour lightly. Remove with a slotted spoon and tip on to kitchen paper to drain. Season the crisps immediately with sea salt, while hot.

**to serve**    When you have deep-fried all the root vegetables, add the parsley sprigs to the oil and deep-fry for about 10 seconds until crisp; remove and drain on kitchen paper. Toss the parsley sprigs with the vegetable crisps and serve in bowls.

**note**    Vegetable crisps are an ideal garnish for main course game dishes.

**variations**    To vary the flavour, sprinkle the hot crisps sparingly with curry powder, paprika, ground cumin or mushroom powder.

# Home-roasted nuts with herbs & sea salt

SERVES 10

*250g skinned almonds*
*250g macadamia nuts*
*250g unsalted peanuts*
*1 tsp chopped thyme*
*1 tsp chopped rosemary, plus*
  *sprigs to garnish*
*sea salt*

**roasting nuts**    Preheat the oven to 190°C (180°C fan oven) Gas 5. Scatter the nuts on a baking tray lined with greaseproof paper and bake for 6–8 minutes until lightly coloured.

**to flavour**    Tip the roasted nuts into a bowl, then add the chopped herbs and season with sea salt while still hot. Toss to mix and allow to cool. Serve garnished with rosemary.

**variations**    Flavour the nuts with spices, such as smoked paprika, cumin seeds or curry powder, rather than herbs.

# Crisp marinated quail eggs

MAKES 12

*12 quail eggs*
*2 tsp white wine vinegar*
*1 tbsp truffle oil*
*salt*

**to finish**
*oil, to deep-fry*
*1 egg*
*1 tbsp milk*
*2 tbsp plain flour*
*50g fresh white breadcrumbs*
    *(preferably one-day old)*
*1 tbsp finely chopped chives*

**poaching quail eggs**    Do this a day ahead. Using a small, serrated knife, carefully remove a quarter of the shell from the wider end of each quail egg and tip the egg out into a small bowl containing 1 tsp wine vinegar. When all the eggs are in the bowl, let them stand for 3–4 minutes. Meanwhile, bring a large, deep pan of water (about 2 litres) to the boil. Add 1 tsp wine vinegar and turn the heat down to a gentle simmer. Stir the water in a circular motion to create a whirlpool, then tip the quail eggs into the centre. Poach for 1 minute, then check by scooping out one egg – it should be firm, but spongy. When ready, lift out the eggs with a slotted spoon and place in a bowl of ice-cold water. After 5 minutes, transfer them to a small bowl, using a slotted spoon. Pour over the truffle oil, cover the bowl tightly with cling film and marinate in the fridge overnight.

**the next day**    Heat the oil in a deep-fat fryer, or deep, heavy saucepan to 180°C. In the meantime, beat the egg with the milk in a small bowl; scatter the flour on a plate; combine the breadcrumbs and chives in a small bowl. Using a small slotted spoon, take a marinated quail egg, shaking off excess truffle oil. Roll in the flour, then dip into the egg mix, and finally roll in the breadcrumbs to coat all over. Deep-fry the eggs in two batches. Immerse in the hot oil and fry for 20–30 seconds only, until crisp and golden brown. Drain on kitchen paper, season with salt and serve, while still hot.

# Curried quail eggs

MAKES 24

*12 quail eggs (at room*
    *temperature)*
*1 tsp mayonnaise*
*pinch of curry powder, to taste*
*salt*

**to finish**
*paprika, to sprinkle*
*12 small coriander sprigs*

**boiling quail eggs**    Bring a small pan of water to the boil. Using a spoon, carefully lower the quail eggs into the water to prevent them cracking and cook for 2 minutes, 20 seconds. Remove with a slotted spoon to a bowl of iced water.

**stuffing quail eggs**    Carefully peel the eggs and halve lengthways. Scoop out the yolks and put into a small bowl. Mash the yolks with the mayonnaise, add the curry powder and season with salt to taste. Spoon the yolk mixture into the whites, using a teaspoon. Sprinkle with paprika and top each stuffed egg with a coriander sprig to serve.

# Button mushroom beignets

SERVES 8–10

**beignet mix**

*300ml milk*

*½ onion, peeled and roughly diced*

*3 tarragon sprigs*

*90g unsalted butter*

*15g plain flour*

*salt and pepper*

*500g button mushrooms, cleaned and finely sliced*

*2 egg yolks, beaten*

**batter**

*100g cornflour*

*150g plain flour*

*2 tsp baking powder*

*400ml sparkling water (approximately)*

**to finish**

*oil, to deep-fry*

*flour, to dust*

**béchamel**  Put the milk and onion into a pan, slowly bring to the boil, then take off the heat. Add the tarragon and leave to infuse for 30 minutes, then strain. Melt 15g butter in a pan, stir in the flour and cook, stirring, over a low heat for 2–3 minutes. Gradually stir in the infused milk, keeping the sauce smooth. Cook the béchamel gently for 10 minutes, stirring frequently. Season with a little salt and transfer to a bowl. Cover the surface with damp greaseproof paper to prevent a skin forming and leave to cool.

**sautéed mushrooms**  Heat half the remaining butter in a large frying pan and sauté half the mushrooms over a high heat for 3–4 minutes until golden. Season, then tip into a colander to drain and cool. Repeat with the remaining mushrooms. (Cooking in two batches ensures the mushrooms fry rather than stew.) When cool, whiz in a food processor for 15–20 seconds until finely diced. Stir into the cooled béchamel; adjust the seasoning. Add the egg yolks and mix until well combined. Cover and chill for 20 minutes.

**shaping the beignets**  Spoon the beignet mixture into a piping bag fitted with a 1cm plain nozzle. Pipe on to a baking tray lined with greaseproof paper in parallel lines, the full length of the tray. (Make sure the tray will fit into your freezer). Freeze the beignet logs until ready to serve.

**batter**  Sift the dry ingredients together into a bowl. Gradually whisk in the water, keeping the mixture smooth and stopping when the batter is a coating consistency. Cover and rest in the fridge for 10 minutes.

**to serve**  Heat the oil for deep-frying to 170–180°C. Cut a frozen beignet log into 6–8cm long batons. Dust the frozen mushroom batons lightly with flour, then dip in the batter to coat and carefully add to the hot oil. Deep-fry for 1–1½ minutes until golden brown. Using a slotted spoon, remove to a plate lined with kitchen paper, season and keep warm. Repeat to cook the rest of the beignets, no more than six at a time. Serve straightaway.

**as a main course**  Use the béchamel and mushrooms as the basis for a pie to serve 4. Sauté 3 skinned, chopped boneless chicken breasts in a little butter until golden and just tender, then stir into the béchamel with the sautéed mushrooms. Spoon into a 1 litre pie dish, brush the rim with water, then cover with a sheet of ready-made puff pastry. Brush with egg wash and bake at 220°C (210°C fan oven) Gas 7 for 15–20 minutes or until golden.

# Leek & red onion tartlets

MAKES 10–12

**pastry cases**
*200g shortcrust pastry (page 156)*
*flour, to dust*

**filling**
*30g unsalted butter*
*2 red onions, peeled and thinly
  sliced*
*1 large leek, split lengthways,
  cleaned and thinly sliced*
*1 garlic clove, peeled and smashed*
*1 tsp chopped sage*
*salt and pepper*

**to finish**
*12 thin slices of chorizo sausage*

**tartlet cases**   Preheat the oven to 200°C (190°C fan oven) Gas 6. Dust the surface lightly with flour and roll out the pastry to a 3–4mm thickness. Cover with cling film and rest for 30 minutes. Cut out discs and use to line a tray of tartlet moulds, 6–8cm in diameter. Prick the bases with a fork, line with greaseproof paper and baking beans, cover with cling film and rest in the fridge for 30 minutes. Remove the cling film and bake the tartlet cases blind for 15–20 minutes until golden brown and crisp. Transfer to a wire rack to cool slightly.

**leek and red onion filling**   Melt the butter in a medium pan over a low heat. Add the red onions, leek, garlic and sage, and season generously with salt and pepper. Stir, then cover and sweat for 10–15 minutes until tender. Drain on kitchen paper.

**to serve**   Spoon the warm leek and onion mixture into the tartlet cases. Roll each chorizo slice into a cornet and place on top. Serve warm.

**variation**   Make the filling as above, then chop the chorizo and stir into the filling. Brush a sheet of filo pastry with melted butter and top with a second filo sheet. Spoon the onion mix along one long edge of the pastry, brush the pastry edges with melted butter and roll up. Place on a baking sheet, tucking the ends underneath, and brush all over with butter. Bake at 210°C (200°C fan oven) Gas 6 for 10–12 minutes. Remove and cut the filo rolls into bite-sized pieces. Serve warm.

# Sweet onion & anchovy pastries

MAKES 32

**pastry bases**

*375g ready-made puff pastry,*
*    thawed if frozen*

**sweet onion topping**

*20g unsalted butter*

*3 white onions, peeled and thinly*
*    sliced*

*2 garlic cloves, peeled and crushed*

*salt*

**to finish**

*about 40 white anchovies in oil,*
*    drained*

*2 tbsp olive oil, to drizzle*

*small flat-leafed parsley sprigs*

**sweet onion topping**    Melt the butter in a medium pan. Add the onions, garlic and a pinch of salt, and fry gently until the onions begin to soften. Turn the heat down to very low and cook, uncovered, for about 40 minutes to allow the onions to caramelise very slowly. Stir from time to time to prevent them burning at the bottom. When ready, they will be deep brown and taste very rich and sweet. Set aside to cool.

**pastry bases**    Preheat the oven to 220°C (210°C fan oven) Gas 7. Roll out the pastry to a 5mm thickness and cut four 20 x 10cm rectangles. Place these on a large baking sheet lined with non-stick baking parchment and prick the pastry all over with a fork. Spoon the sweet onions on to the pastry bases and spread gently and thinly, leaving a 5mm border around the edges. Bake for 12–15 minutes until well risen and golden brown at the crusts. Transfer to a wire rack to cool. Turn the oven down to 200°C (190°C fan oven) Gas 6.

**to assemble**    Arrange the anchovies on the tarts in a criss-cross fashion. Using a very sharp knife, trim away the two shorter crusts on each tart, including the tips of the anchovies. Cut four paper rectangles, slightly larger than the tarts.

**to serve**    Place the tarts on a baking sheet. Lay the paper on top, against the skin of the anchovies. Reheat in the oven for 6–8 minutes until the paper is very hot to the touch; don't let it burn. Remove the paper and lift the tarts on to a board. Cut into small squares to serve as a canapé. Drizzle with olive oil, garnish with parsley and serve warm.

**as a starter, lunch or supper**    The beauty of this dish is that it can be upsized easily. For a starter to serve 8, simply halve the rectangular tarts to give larger squares. For a lunch or supper to serve 4–6, make one large rectangular tart. Cut into generous slices and serve with a leafy salad. The cutting of the pastry is flexible and you can intersperse the anchovies with small black olives to vary the topping.

# Herb-crusted tuna with olive & shallot dressing

MAKES 20–30

**herb-crusted tuna**

*400g fresh tuna mid-cut loin fillet,*
*    cut into 1 or 2 long, 3cm*
*    squared logs*
*4 white anchovies in oil, drained*
*salt*
*3 tbsp olive oil*

**olive and shallot vinaigrette**

*2 large shallots, peeled and finely*
*    diced*
*2 tbsp red wine vinegar*
*10 black olives, pitted and chopped*
*4 tbsp olive oil*

**to finish**

*65g chopped soft herbs (parsley,*
*    basil, chives, tarragon, etc)*
*small salad leaves (watercress,*
*    lamb's lettuce, baby spinach, etc)*

**olive and shallot vinaigrette**    Make this a day ahead if possible. Put the diced shallots into a small bowl and add the wine vinegar. Cover and leave to marinate for a few hours, or preferably overnight. Stir in the chopped olives and olive oil. Cover and refrigerate until needed (for up to a week).

**herb-crusted tuna**    Slit the tuna logs lengthways through to the centre and insert two anchovies in each log, end to end. Press the edges of the tuna together to enclose. Season the surface of the fish all over with salt. Heat a large non-stick frying pan over a high heat, then add the olive oil. When it is almost smoking, add the tuna and sear for 5–8 seconds on each of the 4 sides. Remove and drain on kitchen paper, then allow to rest for 5 minutes. Scatter the chopped herbs on a plate, then roll the tuna logs in the herbs to coat evenly on all sides. Cover and chill for at least 1 hour.

**to serve**    Using a sharp knife, cut the tuna logs into 2cm slices and arrange on cold plates. Spoon over the marinated vinaigrette and scatter small salad leaves around the plates. Serve at room temperature, within an hour of assembling.

**as a main course**    This recipe lends itself easily to upsizing. For a main dish, double the quantities and ask the fishmonger for thicker pieces of tuna loin, ideally 5cm squared logs. Sear for a little longer, 10–15 seconds on each side. Continue as above. Serve the sliced tuna with assorted salad leaves, dressed simply with olive oil, lemon juice, salt and pepper. Drizzle the plate with the shallot and olive vinaigrette. Crushed waxy potatoes flavoured with chives would be a perfect accompaniment.

# Smoked eel pâté with apple & lime

MAKES 16

**pâté**

*150g smoked eel fillet (or smoked*
*   mackerel)*
*75g unsalted butter, softened*
*salt and pepper*
*juice of ½ lime*

**to serve**

*2–3 thin slices of white bread*
*1 Granny Smith apple*
*1 lime*

**smoked eel pâté**   Put the fish into a food processor and process briefly for about 30 seconds, to a paste. Add the softened butter and whiz again for 30 seconds or until smooth. Transfer the mixture to a bowl. Season with salt and pepper, and add half the lime juice, to taste. (Reserve the rest of the lime juice for the apple.)

**melba toast**   Preheat the oven to 190°C (180°C fan oven) Gas 5. Heat the grill (unless you prefer to use the toaster). Toast the bread slices until lightly coloured on both sides. Cool slightly, then remove the crusts and cut each slice horizontally in two. Rub with your fingers to remove loose crumbs. Cut into quarters, then halve each toast to make wafer-thin triangles and place on a baking sheet. Leave in a warm place for 10 minutes to curl, then bake for about 10 minutes until crisp. Allow to cool.

**to serve**   Peel, halve and core the apple. Cut into very thin slices and toss in the reserved lime juice to prevent discolouration. Peel the lime, removing all pith, then cut out the segments – free from the membrane. Place a generous spoonful of fish pâté on each melba toast triangle and top with an apple slice and a lime segment to serve.

**note**   This pâté makes an excellent sandwich filling. Split a crusty baguette lengthways, spread with the smoked eel pâté and top with slices of tomato and ripe avocado. Sandwich together and serve.

# Smoked salmon with horseradish mousse

*Illustrated on page 24*

*Illustrated on page 24*

MAKES 35–40

*500g thinly sliced smoked salmon*

**horseradish mousse**
*150ml double cream, chilled*
*2 tbsp freshly grated horseradish,
    or 3 tbsp ready-made hot
    horseradish sauce*
*squeeze of lemon juice*
*salt and pepper*

**to serve**
*pumpernickel or rye bread*
*lemon wedges (optional)*

**horseradish mousse**   Put a mixing bowl in the freezer to chill thoroughly. Whisk the cream in the chilled bowl until it just starts to thicken, then add the horseradish and a squeeze of lemon juice. Whisk a little more until thick, but not stiff. Add a pinch of salt and several twists of pepper, then set aside to infuse for 15 minutes. Finish by whipping the cream until it is just stiff. Put into a piping bag fitted with a 1cm plain nozzle and refrigerate for about 20 minutes until well chilled.

**smoked salmon rolls**   Cut the smoked salmon into rectangles, 8–10cm wide and 15–20cm long. Tear off a sheet of cling film, slightly longer than the salmon rectangles. Lay a smoked salmon rectangle on the cling film with a long side towards you, leaving at least 3cm cling film free at the front. Pipe a line of horseradish mousse along the salmon, 2cm from the edge closest to you. Lift the cling film overhang and roll the salmon around the horseradish mousse to enclose it and form a roll. Twist the ends of the cling film tightly and tie to form a sausage shape, then place in the freezer. Repeat with the rest of the salmon and horseradish mousse.

**to serve**   Unwrap the frozen salmon rolls and cut into 1cm slices. Allow to defrost at room temperature for about 30 minutes. Serve on squares of pumpernickel or rye bread, with lemon wedges if you like.

## as a starter   *Illustrated on page 25*

*Illustrated on page 25*

Take a large slice of smoked salmon and put a generous spoonful of horseradish mousse on one side. Bring the other half of the salmon over the mousse to enclose it, then flip over and trim the edges to neaten if you like. Serve with rye or pumpernickel bread and lemon wedges.

# Pan-fried chicken livers on garlic croûtes

MAKES 12

garlic croûtes
*12 slices of baguette*
*50g unsalted butter, melted*
*2 garlic cloves, peeled and halved*

pan-fried chicken livers
*100g chicken livers, trimmed*
*1 tbsp groundnut oil*
*1 onion, peeled and finely diced*
*splash of red wine vinegar*
*salt and pepper*

to serve
*1/2 tsp chopped thyme*
*garlic crisps (page 62), optional*

**garlic croûtes**   Preheat the grill. Brush the baguette slices with the butter and rub with a little garlic. Toast on both sides under the hot grill (while you sauté the chicken livers).

**pan-fried chicken livers**   Rinse the chicken livers and pat dry with kitchen paper, then chop roughly and set aside. Heat the oil in a non-stick sauté pan over a low heat, then add the diced onion, cover and sweat for 5–7 minutes until softened. Increase the heat and add the chicken livers. Fry, stirring, over a high heat for 1¹/₂ minutes. Add the wine vinegar and season with salt and pepper to taste.

**to serve**   Spoon the chicken liver mixture on to the warm garlic croûtes and sprinkle with chopped thyme. Scatter a few garlic crisps on top of each one if you like.

**note**   These pan-fried chicken livers are delicious served as a brunch – on a bed of salad leaves lightly dressed with vinaigrette. Accompany with toasted brioche slices and pear chutney (page 157).

# Roasted new potatoes wrapped in Parma ham

MAKES 24

*24 Charlotte potatoes, or other*
*small, waxy potatoes*
*3 garlic cloves, peeled and crushed*
*3 rosemary sprigs*
*1 chicken bouillon cube, crumbled*
*salt*
*12 long slices of Parma or Serrano*
*ham, halved*

**avocado crème fraîche**
*1 ripe avocado*
*2–3 tbsp crème fraîche*
*squeeze of lemon juice*

**to serve**
*2 tbsp olive oil*
*cracked black pepper*
*sea salt*

**par-boiling the potatoes**    Put the potatoes in a saucepan and cover with cold water. Add the garlic, rosemary, chicken bouillon cube and a pinch of salt. Bring to a simmer and cook gently for 15–20 minutes until the potatoes are just tender.

**roasting the potatoes**    Preheat the oven to 210°C (200°C fan oven) Gas 6. Drain the potatoes thoroughly. Wrap each potato tightly in a half-slice of Parma ham, then place on a baking tray. Bake for 6–8 minutes until the Parma ham is lightly caramelised (it will shrink in the oven to form a tight wrap around the potatoes). Leave to cool slightly.

**avocado crème fraîche**    Prepare this while the potatoes are in the oven. Peel, halve and stone the avocado, then roughly chop the flesh. Put into a blender with 2 tsp cold water and whiz until smooth. Transfer to a bowl and fold in the crème fraîche. Add the lemon juice and season with salt to taste.

**to serve**    Using a sharp knife, cut the Parma-wrapped potatoes into chunky slices, or simply cut in half. Arrange on a platter and drizzle with the olive oil, cracked black pepper and sea salt. Provide cocktail sticks and serve the avocado crème fraîche as a dip.

**note**    If you prepare the avocado crème fraîche in advance, push the stone into the mixture, cover the bowl and refrigerate. The helps to prevent discolouration.

**as a starter or main course** Use the roasted Parma-wrapped potatoes as the basis for a warm salad. Toss the sliced potatoes with 1 or 2 handfuls of baby sorrel or spinach leaves and 1 sliced avocado. Drizzle with vinaigrette to serve.

# Foie gras parfait with poppy seed crisps

MAKES 24–30

**parfait**

*100g chicken livers, trimmed and
roughly chopped*

*100g foie gras, trimmed and
roughly chopped*

*3 eggs, beaten*

*100ml port*

*100ml Madeira*

*1 shallot, peeled and finely
chopped*

*1 bay leaf*

*1 thyme sprig*

*200g butter, melted*

*salt and pepper*

**poppy seed crisps**

*2 sheets filo pastry*

*50g unsalted butter, melted*

*1 tsp poppy seeds*

**foie gras parfait**    Take the chicken livers, foie gras and eggs out of the fridge an hour ahead to bring to room temperature. Preheat the oven to 160°C (150°C fan oven) Gas 2½. Put the port, Madeira, shallot, bay leaf and thyme into a pan and bring to the boil. Let bubble until reduced by two-thirds, then take off the heat and discard the herbs; let cool slightly. Meanwhile, gently warm the chicken livers and foie gras in a pan over a low heat for 30–45 seconds until lukewarm. Tip into a blender, add the reduced liquor and eggs and whiz until smooth. With the motor running, slowly add the melted butter and blend for 2 minutes. Season with ½ tsp salt and 6 turns of the pepper mill. Pass through a fine sieve into a bowl.

**cooking the parfait**    Spoon the parfait mixture into a greased medium soufflé dish. Stand in a shallow roasting tin and surround with warm water to come halfway up the sides. Cook in the oven for 35–45 minutes or until just firm on the surface. Remove from the oven and leave to cool in the bain-marie, then take out, cover and refrigerate.

**poppy seed crisps**    Increase the oven temperature to 200°C (190°C fan oven) Gas 6. Lay the filo sheets on a baking sheet lined with baking parchment. Brush with butter, sprinkle with poppy seeds and season with salt. Bake for about 8 minutes until golden. Transfer to a wire rack to cool.

**to serve**    Break the filo pastry into irregular pieces. Spoon or pipe a small mound of parfait on to half of the poppy seed crisps. Top each one with another filo crisp and serve.

**note**    This parfait is also excellent as a starter – with toasted brioche or walnut bread, cornichons and a chutney, such as pear chutney (page 157).

# quick & easy

Cep, artichoke & broad bean salad

Aubergine roasted couscous

Sweetcorn fritters with crisp bacon & soft cheese

Minestrone

Roasted spring carrots with star anise & tarragon

Roasted goat's cheese & red pepper salad

Soft polenta with Gruyère & mushroom fricassée

Scallops with basil oil & crisp Serrano ham

Oysters with shallot vinaigrette & watercress

Mussels in a creamy sauce with basil

Mackerel with sweet & sour pepper jus

Sardine frittata with spring onions

Roasted skate wing with crispy capers

Seared salmon with cauliflower purée

Poached cod with chive scrambled eggs

Warm chicken, baby spinach & mozzarella salad

Warm salad of rocket & lamb with garlic crisps

# Cep, artichoke & broad bean salad

SERVES 4

*2 large globe artichokes*

*1 quantity pickling marinade*
  *(see page 10)*

*125g podded broad beans*

*300g ceps or shiitake mushrooms*

*2 tbsp olive oil*

*1 shallot, peeled and finely diced*

*salt*

**mushroom and thyme vinaigrette**

*300ml olive oil*

*120g shiitake mushrooms, roughly*
  *chopped*

*1 garlic clove, peeled*

*3–4 thyme sprigs*

*salt*

*½ shallot, peeled and finely*
  *chopped*

*100ml balsamic vinegar*

**to finish**

*120g rocket or baby spinach leaves*

*1 tbsp olive oil*

*1 tsp balsamic vinegar*

**mushroom and thyme vinaigrette**    Make this in advance. Heat a small frying pan over a high heat, then add 2 tbsp olive oil. When hot, add the mushrooms, garlic, thyme and a pinch of salt. Cook, stirring occasionally, for 4–5 minutes until the mushrooms are brown in colour, then add the shallot. Cook over a low heat for a minute or two, until the shallot is lightly browned. Take the pan off the heat and add the balsamic vinegar to deglaze, scraping up the sediment on the bottom of the pan. Tip the mixture into a blender or food processor, add the remaining olive oil and whiz for 1 minute until smooth. Pour into a screw-topped jar and set aside to cool, then refrigerate until needed.

**artichokes**    Pull off the outer leaves from the artichokes to reveal the hearts, then remove the hairy choke at the base of each one. Bring the pickling marinade to a simmer in a pan, then add the artichoke hearts and simmer for about 5 minutes until just tender. Take off the heat and leave to cool in the marinade.

**broad beans**    Add the broad beans to a pan of boiling salted water and blanch for 1½–2 minutes until tender. Drain and immediately refresh in iced water. Drain and slip the broad beans out of their skins.

**to assemble**    Cut the cooked artichoke hearts into 2cm dice. Cut the ceps or shiitake mushrooms into 5mm thick slices. Heat a non-stick pan over a high heat and add the 2 tbsp olive oil. When hot, add the artichokes and mushrooms, season with salt, and sauté for 2–3 minutes until light brown in colour. Turn off the heat and add the finely diced shallot and broad beans. Toss to mix and leave in the pan for 2 minutes to warm through.

**to serve**    Dress the salad leaves with the olive oil and balsamic vinegar. Pile the warm salad on to warmed plates and drizzle with the mushroom and thyme vinaigrette. Top with the salad leaves and serve.

# Aubergine roasted couscous

SERVES 6

*1 aubergine, about 500g*
*100ml olive oil*
*2 tsp ground cumin*
*250g couscous*
*3 garlic cloves, peeled and crushed*
*300ml hot chicken stock (page 156)*
*2 tomatoes, skinned, deseeded and*
*   roughly chopped*
*15 basil leaves, shredded*
*salt and pepper*
*4 large basil leaves, deep-fried*
*   if preferred, to garnish*

**preparing the aubergine**    Peel the skin from the aubergine, then cut the flesh into 1cm cubes. Heat a large heavy-based frying pan over a high heat, then add a third of the olive oil. When hot, add the aubergine cubes and cumin. Fry, stirring frequently, for 2–3 minutes until the aubergine is golden brown and tender. Remove with a slotted spoon and drain on kitchen paper.

**pan-roasting the couscous**    Reheat the pan, then add the rest of the olive oil. When very hot, add the couscous with the garlic and fry, turning frequently, for 2–3 minutes until golden brown.

**to assemble**    Add the stock to the couscous with the aubergine dice, tomatoes and shredded basil. Toss to mix, then remove from the heat and cover tightly. Leave to stand for 5 minutes.

**to serve**    Uncover and fork through the couscous. Taste and adjust the seasoning. Divide the couscous among warmed plates or bowls and garnish with deep-fried or fresh basil leaves. Serve at once.

**as a main course**    Season 4 lamb chump chops and cook on an oiled griddle or barbecue for 4–5 minutes each side until well browned, but still pink inside. Serve with the warm aubergine roasted couscous.

# Sweetcorn fritters with crisp bacon & soft cheese

SERVES 4

sweetcorn fritters

*100g plain flour*
*2 tsp baking powder*
*100ml milk*
*2 tbsp drained canned sweetcorn*
*pinch of salt*
*2 tbsp vegetable oil, to fry*

to assemble

*8 slices of smoked bacon*
*100g soft goat's cheese*

**sweetcorn fritter batter**   Sift the flour and baking powder together into a bowl, make a well in the middle and add the milk, sweetcorn and salt. Whisk together until evenly blended, then cover and leave to rest for 15 minutes.

**oven-crisped bacon**   Preheat the oven to 220°C (210°C fan oven) Gas 7. Lay the bacon slices side by side on a sturdy baking sheet. Place another heavy baking sheet on top to keep them flat and cook in the oven for 8–12 minutes until crisp. Drain on kitchen paper.

**to cook the fritters**   Heat a large non-stick frying pan over a medium heat and add the vegetable oil. When hot, cook the sweetcorn fritters. Spoon in 2 tbsp sweetcorn batter for each fritter, spacing them well apart. Fry for 1–2 minutes until golden underneath, then carefully turn, using a spatula, and cook the other side for a minute or two until brown and crisp. Drain on kitchen paper.

**to serve**   Cut each sweetcorn fritter in half and arrange on serving plates with a spoonful of soft goat's cheese. Top with the crisp bacon slices and serve.

### as a main course

Omit the bacon and cheese. Double the batter quantity and cook larger fritters (4 tbsp each). Flatten 8 chicken thighs and fry, skin-side down, in a little oil for 8–10 minutes, then turn and fry for 2–3 minutes or until golden and cooked through. Drain a 160g can sweetcorn and heat with 200ml chicken stock for 3 minutes, then purée in a blender and pass through a sieve. Serve the chicken thighs on the sweetcorn fritters with the sweetcorn purée and a watercress salad.

# Minestrone

SERVES 4

*1 tbsp olive oil*

*1 garlic clove, peeled*

*25g onion, peeled and diced*

*50g trimmed leek, diced*

*50g carrot, peeled and diced*

*50g celery, trimmed and diced*

*2 thyme sprigs*

*2 bay leaves*

*salt and pepper*

*2 tsp tomato purée*

*100g peeled white potato, diced and rinsed*

*20 strands spaghetti strands, broken into 2cm lengths*

*2 tomatoes, deseeded and diced*

*8 basil leaves, chopped*

**basil oil**

*20g basil leaves*

*50ml olive oil*

**minestrone**　　Heat the olive oil in a medium pan with the garlic clove. Add the onion, leek, carrot and celery with the thyme, bay leaves and a pinch of salt. Stir, then cover and sweat over a low heat for 5–6 minutes until the vegetables have softened. Add the tomato purée, potato and 1 litre water. Bring to the boil, then add the pasta. Bring to a simmer, skim the surface and cook on a low heat for 10–12 minutes or until the potato and pasta are cooked. Discard the garlic clove.

**basil oil**　　Meanwhile, blanch the 20g basil leaves in boiling salted water for 25 seconds; drain well. Whiz the basil in a blender with the olive oil for 30–40 seconds until smooth.

**to finish**　　Stir the diced tomatoes and chopped basil into the soup, then taste and adjust the seasoning. Ladle into warmed deep bowls and sprinkle with the basil oil. Serve straightaway.

**note**　　For a simple finish, omit the basil oil and serve the minestrone scattered with freshly grated Parmesan and small basil leaves. For a more substantial soup, to serve as a meal in itself, replace the spaghetti with a large handful of penne or other chunky pasta, or serve each portion topped with a handful of cheesy croûtons.

# Roasted spring carrots with star anise & tarragon

SERVES 4

*600g baby spring carrots or other
    thin, small carrots*
*45g unsalted butter*
*4 star anise*
*salt and pepper*
*large pinch of sugar*
*100ml chicken stock or vegetable
    nage (page 156)*
*10g tarragon leaves, roughly torn*

**pan-roasting the carrots**    Peel the carrots and trim them down to an
even size, leaving on a tuft of the green stalk. Place a large non-stick frying
pan over a medium heat. When hot, add the butter together with the star
anise. As soon as the butter starts foaming, add the carrots and season
with salt. Allow the carrots to roast slowly in the butter for 7–8 minutes,
rolling them from time to time to ensure they turn golden on all sides.

**caramelising the carrots**    Drain off the excess butter from the pan,
then sprinkle the sugar over the carrots and turn for a few moments to
glaze on all sides. Pour in the stock and allow to bubble slowly until it is
reduced down to a sticky aromatic glaze and the carrots are just cooked –
they should retain a slight bite.

**to finish**    Scatter over the torn tarragon leaves and check the seasoning.
Divide the carrots among warmed plates and drizzle with a little of the
glaze. Retain the star anise as a garnish. Serve at once.

**note**    If the glaze is too sticky, thin with a little hot stock or water
before spooning over the carrots to serve.

**as a main course** Season 2 pork fillets (tenderloins) and brown in a little oil in a frying pan over a high heat. Transfer to a roasting tin and roast at 200°C (190°C fan oven) Gas 5 for 15–20 minutes or until tender and cooked through; rest for 5–10 minutes. Cook 12 baby turnips in boiling salted water for 7–8 minutes until tender; drain and toss with butter. Halve the pork fillets and serve on the roasted carrots with the turnips and glaze.

# Roasted goat's cheese & red pepper salad

SERVES 4

**roasted peppers**

*2 red peppers*

*2 tbsp olive oil*

*salt and pepper*

**roasted goat's cheese**

*2 tsp chopped walnuts*

*2 tsp chopped hazelnuts*

*4 tbsp breadcrumbs*

*2 egg yolks*

*1 tbsp milk*

*4 slices firm goat's cheese log or
    4 small whole cheeses, about
    60g each*

*2 tbsp plain flour, to dust*

**to serve**

*20 black olives, pitted*

*100g mixed salad leaves (frisée,
    lamb's lettuce, radicchio etc)*

*2 tbsp vinaigrette (page 157)*

**roasting the peppers**    Preheat the oven to 220°C (210°C fan oven) Gas 7. Cut the red peppers in half and remove the seeds and white membrane. Brush all over with olive oil, season with salt and pepper and place on a baking tray. Roast in the oven for 15–20 minutes until softened and lightly coloured. Leave to cool.

**roasting the goat's cheese**    Combine the chopped nuts with the breadcrumbs and scatter on a plate. Beat the egg yolks with the milk (to make an egg wash). Dust the goat's cheese with flour to coat lightly all over. One at a time, dip into the egg wash, then into the crumb nut mixture to coat evenly all over. Place the crumb-coated goat's cheeses on a baking tray lined with greaseproof paper. Bake for 6–8 minutes, turning once or twice, until the coating is crisp and golden brown.

**to serve**    Cut each roasted pepper half into quarters and arrange on warmed plates with the roasted goat's cheese and olives. Dress the salad leaves with vinaigrette, season and serve alongside.

# Soft polenta with Gruyère & mushroom fricassée

SERVES 4

**polenta**

*500ml chicken stock or vegetable
 nage (page 156)*
*salt and pepper*
*200g polenta (see note)*
*3 tbsp unsalted butter*
*100g Gruyère cheese, grated, plus
 extra to serve*

**mushroom fricassée**

*150g wild mushrooms, cleaned
 and trimmed*
*2 tbsp olive oil*
*2 garlic cloves, peeled and cracked*
*1 tbsp chopped parsley*
*squeeze of lemon juice, to taste*

**to cook the polenta**  Bring the stock to the boil in a large saucepan and add a large pinch of salt. Slowly pour in the polenta, whisking continuously as you do so to prevent lumps forming. Cook the polenta over a low heat, stirring frequently, for about 15–20 minutes until the stock is absorbed and the polenta no longer tastes raw.

**mushroom fricassée**  Halve or slice any larger mushrooms; leave small ones whole. About 5 minutes before the polenta is likely to be cooked, heat the olive oil in a frying pan and add the cracked garlic cloves. As the oil starts to smoke, add the mushrooms and immediately season them with salt and pepper. Cook, stirring occasionally, for 2–3 minutes, then add the chopped parsley and lemon juice. Discard the garlic. Tip the mushrooms out on to a plate, cover and keep warm.

**to finish**  Once the polenta is cooked out, fold in the butter and grated cheese, then season with salt and pepper to taste.

**to serve**  Spoon the polenta into the centre of four warmed plates and top with the mushroom fricassée. Sprinkle with grated Gruyère and serve.

**note**  Buy standard polenta, not the quick-cook 'instant polenta'.

**as a main course**  Make the polenta and mushroom fricassée as above. Season 8 oven-ready quail. Heat an ovenproof frying pan or shallow flameproof casserole over a high heat until smoking. Add 2 tbsp oil, then the quail. Fry, turning with tongs, until lightly caramelised all over, then roast in the oven at 230°C (220°C fan oven) Gas 8 for 5–6 minutes for medium-rare, or 8–10 minutes for well done. Rest for 10 minutes. Take the quail legs and breasts off the bone and serve on the polenta. Spoon the mushroom fricassée alongside.

## as a canapé
Crush the dried Serrano ham into rough crumbs. Skewer the hot pan-roasted scallops on to cocktail sticks, putting two or three on each stick. Quickly roll in the crisp ham crumbs and arrange on a plate drizzled with basil oil for dipping.

# Scallops with basil oil & crisp Serrano ham

SERVES 6

*4 slices of Serrano ham*
*40 queen scallops, shelled and*
  *cleaned*
*salt*
*1 tbsp olive oil*
**basil oil**
*40g basil leaves*
*100ml olive oil*

**basil oil**    Prepare this in advance. Bring 1 litre water to the boil in a pan with 20g salt added. Blanch the basil leaves for 25 seconds, then remove and drain well. Put into a blender with the 100ml olive oil and whiz for 30–40 seconds until smooth. Pour the basil oil into a small jar and refrigerate. Bring to room temperature when ready to use.

**Serrano ham**    Preheat the oven to 190°C (180°C fan oven) Gas 5. Lay the ham slices in a single layer on a baking sheet lined with non-stick baking parchment. Cover with another sheet of baking parchment and place another tray on top, to ensure the ham dries in flat sheets. Put into the oven for 10–14 minutes until crisp and dry, with little colouring. To check, break off a small piece and rub gently on a cool surface, then check it is crisp. Transfer the ham to a plate lined with kitchen paper and let cool.

**pan-roasting scallops**    Pat the scallops dry on kitchen paper and season with salt. Heat a non-stick frying pan over a medium-high heat and add the 1 tbsp olive oil. When the oil is very hot but not smoking, add the scallops and cook for 25–30 seconds only. Gently move the delicate scallops in the pan with a wooden spoon as they cook, to sear evenly all over. Carefully transfer the cooked scallops to a plate lined with kitchen paper to drain.

**to serve**    Quickly streak the warmed plates with the basil oil and arrange the warm scallops on top. Break the crisp ham into pieces and scatter over the scallops. Serve immediately.

# Oysters with shallot vinaigrette & watercress

SERVES 4

*20 oysters*

shallot vinaigrette

*2 large shallots, peeled and finely*
*    diced*
*80ml finest red wine vinegar*
*    (preferably Cabernet Sauvignon)*
*80ml olive oil*
*salt*

to serve

*rock salt*
*handful of watercress leaves*

**shallot vinaigrette**    Make this a day in advance. In a small bowl, combine the shallots, wine vinegar and olive oil. Add a pinch of salt, then cover and leave to infuse at room temperature overnight.

**to open the oysters**    Hold an oyster in a folded cloth on a surface with the flatter shell up and the hinge pointing towards you. Force the tip of an oyster knife into the hinge of the shell, then carefully move it from side to side to work the shells apart – this takes some effort. Slide the blade of the knife along the inside of the upper shell until you come to the muscle, which attaches the oyster to the shell. Cut through this to detach the top shell. Holding the oyster over a bowl to catch any juices, lift off the top shell. Carefully run the blade of the knife under the oyster to loosen it, then clean away any broken fragments of shell.

**to serve**    Whisk the vinaigrette to re-combine. Line the serving plates with a bed of rock salt and arrange five oysters on each one. Spoon ½ tsp of the shallot vinaigrette over each oyster. Spoon the rest of the vinaigrette into four tiny serving dishes and place in the centre of each plate (for guests to help themselves). Arrange the watercress leaves on top of the oysters and serve.

**note**    Always buy a few extra oysters, as you cannot be sure that they will all be perfect. As you open each oyster, check that the flesh has a clean smell of the sea. If in any doubt, discard.

# Mussels in a creamy sauce with basil

SERVES 4

*1kg fresh mussels in shells*
*75ml olive oil*
*1 onion, peeled and roughly*
  *chopped*
*1 celery stick, trimmed and roughly*
  *chopped*
*1 leek, white only, halved and*
  *roughly chopped*
*4 garlic cloves, peeled and cracked*
*400ml white wine*
*75ml double cream*
*squeeze of lemon juice, to taste*
*salt and pepper*
*large handful of basil leaves,*
  *chopped if preferred*

**to clean mussels**   Rinse the mussels under cold running water, scrubbing the shells thoroughly to remove sand and grit. Pull off the 'beards' from the side of the shell. Tap any open mussels sharply with the back of a knife and discard any that do not close. Give the mussels a final rinse before cooking.

**to cook the mussels**   Heat a large pan (one that will take all the mussels and has a tight-fitting lid) and add 1 tbsp olive oil. Add the onion, celery, leek and garlic. Stir, then cover and sweat over a low heat for 8–10 minutes until soft. Add the wine, increase the heat and let bubble until reduced by two-thirds. Add the mussels, cover tightly and steam until all (or nearly all) of the shells have opened. Start checking after 3 minutes. Drain the mussels, reserving the liquor, and discard any that remain closed. Tip the mussels into a large bowl; cover to prevent them drying out.

**for the sauce**   Pour the cooking liquor into a small pan and bubble vigorously over a high heat until reduced by half. Add the cream, then pour into a blender. With the motor running, slowly add the remaining 60ml olive oil. When it is amalgamated, add a squeeze of lemon juice and season with salt and pepper to taste.

**to serve**   Add the cream sauce and basil to the mussels and toss to mix. Serve in large bowls, with plenty of fresh bread.

**as a pasta dish**   Skin, deseed and chop 4 ripe, flavourful tomatoes; set aside. Cook the mussels as above, then drain and remove from their shells while the cooking liquor is reducing. Meanwhile, cook 400g linguine in plenty of boiling salted water until al dente. After whizzing the cream into the reduced liquor with the lemon juice and seasoning, return to the pan and add the shelled mussels and chopped tomatoes. Warm through very gently for a minute or two if necessary, then divide among serving bowls. Drain the pasta, add to the bowls and serve at once.

# Mackerel with sweet & sour pepper jus

SERVES 4

*4 mackerel fillets, about 100g each*
*1 tbsp olive oil*
*salt and pepper*

**pepper jus**
*3 red peppers*
*1 yellow pepper*
*large pinch of sugar*
*1 tbsp double cream*
*juice of 1/2 lemon*
*20g unsalted butter, chilled and*
*  diced*
*1 tsp chopped marjoram or*
*  oregano*

**preparing the mackerel**    Check over the mackerel fillets and remove any small bones with tweezers. Score the skin with a sharp knife in close parallel lines.

**preparing the peppers**    Using a swivel vegetable peeler, remove the skin from 1 red pepper and the yellow pepper. Halve these peppers and remove the core, seeds and membrane, then cut the flesh into 5mm dice and set aside. Halve, core and deseed the other peppers and remove the white membrane.

**pepper jus**    Whiz the red pepper halves in a blender (or process in a juicer) and pass through a fine sieve. Put the pepper jus into a pan with the diced peppers, sugar, cream, a pinch of salt and the lemon juice. Bring to the boil and bubble to reduce by two-thirds. Lower the heat and whisk in the cold butter, a piece at a time. Stir in the chopped marjoram, check the seasoning and keep warm.

**to cook the mackerel**    Heat a large non-stick frying pan over a medium heat. Season the mackerel fillets with salt and pepper. Add the olive oil to the pan and, when hot, place the seasoned mackerel fillets in the pan, skin-side down. Fry for 3 minutes, then turn the fillets over and fry for 1 minute or until the mackerel is just cooked.

**to serve**    Place the mackerel fillets in the centre of warmed plates and surround with the warm pepper jus. Serve at once.

**as a main course**    Bake a whole sea bass, about 1kg, to serve with the sweet and sour pepper juice. Season the cavity of the cleaned fish and stuff with 1/4 lime and 1/2 fennel bulb, chopped. Rub the skin with olive oil, season with salt and pepper and wrap in foil. Place in a roasting tin and bake at 200°C (190°C fan oven) Gas 6 for 25–30 minutes or until the fish comes away easily from the bone. Serve with the sweet and sour pepper jus.

# Sardine frittata with spring onions

SERVES 4

*8 sardines, about 100g each,*
   *preferably scaled and cleaned*
   *with heads removed*
*400g potato (King Edward or*
   *Desirée)*
*25g unsalted butter*
*1 garlic clove, peeled and crushed*
*salt and pepper*
*½ red onion, peeled and thinly*
   *sliced*
*4 large eggs*
*1 tbsp plain flour, to dust*
*2 tbsp olive oil*
*2 spring onions, trimmed and*
   *roughly chopped*
*100ml soured cream*

**preparing the sardines**    If the fishmonger hasn't already done so for you, clean the sardines, removing the scales, heads and entrails. Rinse the fish thoroughly and pat dry with kitchen paper. Lightly score the skin side with a small sharp knife. Preheat the oven to 220°C (210°C fan oven) Gas 7.

**to cook the potatoes**    Peel and thinly slice the potato. Heat a 23–25cm frying pan (suitable for use in the oven). When hot, add the butter followed by the garlic. When the butter is sizzling, add the potatoes and season with salt and pepper. Sauté for 3–4 minutes, turning the potato slices frequently until lightly browned on both sides. Add the red onion and sauté for a further 2 minutes.

**making the frittata**    Break the eggs into a bowl, season with salt and pepper and whisk lightly with a fork. Pour over the sautéed potato slices and place in the oven for 3–5 minutes until the egg is just set.

**pan-frying sardines**    Season the fish with salt and pepper, then dust with flour. Heat a non-stick frying pan and, when hot, add the olive oil. Lay the sardines in the pan and fry for about 1 minute on each side, or according to size, until golden brown and just cooked.

**to serve**    Slide the frittata out of the pan on to a board and cut into 4 wedges. Place one on each warmed plate and scatter over the chopped spring onions. Top with a generous spoonful of soured cream and serve.

**note**    This frittata can be made in advance and served at room temperature, cut into small squares, as a canapé.

# Roasted skate wing with crispy capers

SERVES 4

2 skate wings, about 500g each,
   skinned, trimmed and halved
salt and pepper
4 tbsp olive oil
3–4 rosemary sprigs
100g capers
50g butter
juice of 1/2 lemon
3 tbsp chopped parsley
4 tbsp aged balsamic vinegar
   (see note)

**to cook the skate**    Preheat the oven to 220°C (210°C fan oven) Gas 7. Pat the skate portions dry with kitchen paper and season both sides with salt and pepper. Heat a large non-stick frying pan (suitable for use in the oven) over a high heat. When hot, add 2 tbsp of the olive oil and the rosemary sprigs. Put the skate wings in the pan, thickest side down, and fry for 2 minutes until golden brown. Turn the fish and cook for a further 2 minutes. Transfer the pan to the oven for 2 minutes to finish cooking.

**to finish**    Move the fish to a warmed plate to rest for a few minutes; discard the rosemary. Meanwhile, drain off the oil from the pan, then add 2 tbsp fresh olive oil and place over a high heat. When the oil is very hot, add the capers and shallow-fry for about 30–45 seconds until crispy. Remove the capers with a slotted spoon and drain on kitchen paper. Add the butter to the pan and, when it starts to foam, stir in the lemon juice.

**to serve**    Arrange the skate on warmed plates, scatter over the crispy capers and chopped parsley and spoon over the lemon butter sauce. Drizzle the plates with the balsamic vinegar to serve.

**note**    If you do not have any aged balsamic, use twice the amount of standard balsamic vinegar and bubble over a medium-high heat to reduce by half – until syrupy.

**as a main course**    Simply double the quantities and serve with samphire or spinach and creamy mash. Alternatively, make the recipe as above and serve each skate wing portion topped with a few slices of crispy belly pork (page 98); accompany with a portion of apple and frisée salad and creamy mash.

# Seared salmon with cauliflower purée

*Illustrated on page 56*

**SERVES 4**

*4 thick salmon fillets, about 100g
  each, skinned*
*salt and black pepper*
*2 tbsp olive oil*
*squeeze of lemon juice*

**cauliflower purée**
*500g cauliflower, roughly chopped*
*500ml milk*
*150ml double cream*
*salt and white pepper*

**to garnish**
*chervil sprigs*

**preparing the salmon**   Check over the salmon and remove any small bones with tweezers.

**cauliflower purée**   Put the cauliflower, milk and cream into a medium saucepan. Add a pinch of salt and bring to a simmer. Simmer gently for 10–12 minutes until the cauliflower is very tender and the milk has reduced by half. Drain the cauliflower, reserving the liquor. Put the cauliflower into a blender with 150ml of the cooking liquor and whiz to a purée. If necessary, blend in a little more liquor to obtain a thick pouring consistency. Pass through a fine sieve into a bowl, pressing the cauliflower purée through with the back of a ladle or spoon. Season with salt and white pepper to taste and keep warm.

**pan-frying the salmon**   Season the fillets with salt and black pepper. Heat  a non-stick frying pan over a high heat, and add the olive oil. When hot, add the salmon fillets and cook for 2–3 minutes on each side until lightly caramelised around the edges. Drain on kitchen paper and finish with a squeeze of lemon juice.

**to serve**   Flake the salmon and arrange on each warmed plate. Spoon a generous portion of cauliflower purée alongside. Garnish with chervil and grind a little black pepper over the salmon to serve.

## as main course fish cakes   *Illustrated on page 57*

Omit the cauliflower purée. Cook the salmon fillets as above, cool, then flake. Boil 400g potatoes in salted water until tender, then drain and dry over a low heat. Mash or press through a sieve into a bowl. Add the flaked salmon, 2 medium egg yolks, juice of 1/2 lemon, 2 tbsp softened butter, 2 tbsp chopped chives, 2 tsp chopped capers (optional) and plenty of seasoning. Mix well, then shape into 8 cakes and dust with flour. Dip into beaten egg, then into fresh white breadcrumbs to coat. Heat 4 tbsp oil in a large frying pan and fry the fish cakes until crisp and golden, turning once. Drain on kitchen paper and serve with pickled cauliflower (page 10) and a watercress salad.

# Poached cod with chive scrambled eggs

SERVES 4

*200g cod fillet, skinned*

*500ml milk*

*1 tsp sea salt*

*½ onion, peeled*

*2 garlic cloves, peeled*

*1 bay leaf*

*1 thyme sprig*

*5 black peppercorns*

scrambled eggs

*6 eggs*

*salt and pepper*

*40g unsalted butter*

*4 tbsp double cream*

*1 tbsp chopped chives*

to serve

*4 slices of white bread or brioche,*
  *freshly toasted*

**poaching the cod**    Check over the cod and remove any residual bones with tweezers. Put the milk, salt, onion, garlic, bay leaf, thyme and peppercorns into a wide saucepan. Bring to a simmer, turn off the heat and allow to infuse for 10 minutes. Add the cod to the infused liquor and simmer very gently for 6–8 minutes or until just cooked (the surface of the liquor should barely move). When ready, carefully remove the cod to a warmed plate and keep warm.

**scrambling the eggs**    Prepare these while the cod is poaching. Beat the eggs with a little salt and pepper. Melt the butter in a non-stick saucepan over a low heat. Pour in the eggs and stir constantly with a wooden spoon until almost scrambled. Stir in the cream and three-quarters of the chives and take off the heat. Check the seasoning and immediately remove the scrambled eggs from the pan to prevent further cooking.

**to serve**    Put a slice of hot toast on each warmed plate and pile the scrambled eggs on top. Divide the warm cod into chunky flakes and arrange on the eggs. Sprinkle with the rest of the chives and serve.

**note**    As an alternative, use filleted haddock. For a more substantial fish course, double the quantities and serve with new potatoes tossed with melted butter and chopped dill.

**as a main course** Omit the avocado. Pan-fry 4 whole chicken breasts for 3–5 minutes with the red onion until golden. Transfer to a roasting tin and cook at 200°C (190°C fan oven) for 20 minutes. Top with the mozzarella and almonds; bake for a further 5 minutes or until the chicken is cooked. Meanwhile cook the spinach in a covered pan for 30 seconds or until starting to wilt. Toss with the red onion and pile on to plates. Top with the sun-dried tomatoes, basil, bacon and chicken.

# Warm chicken, baby spinach & mozzarella salad

SERVES 4

*12 inner chicken breast fillets, or
2 whole skinless breast fillets*

*salt and pepper*

*4 slices smoked bacon*

*40g split or flaked almonds*

*1 large ripe avocado*

*lemon juice, to sprinkle*

*2 tbsp olive oil*

*½ red onion, peeled and finely
diced*

*200g baby spinach leaves, washed*

*8 boccacini mozzarella, halved, or
1 large buffalo mozzarella, sliced*

*6 basil leaves, sliced*

*12 sun-dried tomatoes, cut into
strips*

*4 tbsp vinaigrette (page 157)*

**preparing the chicken**    If using whole breast fillets, cut crossways into slices. Season the chicken with salt and pepper.

**the bacon, almonds and avocado**    Preheat the oven to 220°C (210°C fan oven) Gas 7. Lay the bacon slices side by side on a sturdy baking sheet. Place another heavy baking sheet on top to keep them flat and cook in the oven for 8–12 minutes until crisp; drain on kitchen paper. Scatter the almonds on a baking sheet and toast in the oven for 5–6 minutes until lightly golden. Halve, stone and peel the avocado, then slice and toss in a little lemon juice to prevent discolouration; set aside.

**pan-frying the chicken**    Heat a large non-stick frying pan or wok until smoking hot. Add the olive oil, then the chicken and sauté for 2–3 minutes until lightly coloured. Add the diced red onion and cook over a low heat for a further 5–6 minutes until the chicken is cooked and the onion is softened, stirring frequently to ensure it doesn't burn.

**assembling the salad**    Add the spinach to the pan, then immediately take off the heat and add the mozzarella, almonds, basil and sun-dried tomatoes. Toss and stir continuously until the spinach starts to wilt and the cheese begins to melt. Check the seasoning.

**to serve**    Divide the warm salad among warmed plates and drizzle with the vinaigrette. Arrange the avocado slices and bacon on top, breaking the crisp bacon into smaller pieces if you like. Serve immediately, with warm crusty bread.

# Warm salad of rocket & lamb with garlic crisps

SERVES 4

*400g lamb fillet (ideally, the inner*
   *fillet from the saddle), trimmed*
*salt and pepper*
*2 tbsp vegetable oil*

**garlic crisps**
*16 large garlic cloves*
*400ml milk*
*vegetable oil, to deep-fry*

**rocket salad**
*200g wild rocket leaves*
*1 tbsp olive oil*
*1 tbsp balsamic vinegar*

**preparing the lamb**    Preheat the oven to 210°C (200°C fan oven) Gas 6. Season the lamb fillets with salt and pepper and set aside.

**garlic crisps**    Cut the garlic cloves into wafer-thin slices and put into a small pan with half of the milk. Bring to the boil, then strain off and discard the milk. Add the rest of the milk and repeat the process. Drain the garlic in a fine strainer and rinse under cold running water to remove all milk residue. Drain and pat dry on kitchen paper. Heat the oil in a deep-fat fryer or other suitable deep pan to 150°C. When hot, fry the garlic slivers in two small batches for 5–6 seconds or until they just start to colour. Remove with a slotted spoon and drain on kitchen paper.

**roasting the lamb fillet**    Heat a frying pan with a metal handle (suitable for use in the oven) until smoking hot then add the 2 tbsp vegetable oil. Add the lamb fillet and sear, turning, for about 2 minutes until lightly golden on all sides. Place the pan in the hot oven and roast the lamb for 2–3 minutes for medium rare, or 3–5 minutes for medium. Remove from the oven and allow the meat to rest for 10 minutes.

**rocket salad**    Put the rocket leaves into a bowl and dress with the olive oil and a third of the balsamic vinegar. Season with a pinch of salt and a twist of black pepper.

**to serve**    Thinly slice the lamb and arrange on serving plates. Scatter the rocket salad and garlic crisps over the meat and drizzle with the remaining balsamic vinegar. Serve at once.

**as a main course** Buy 2 French-trimmed racks of lamb, each with 3–4 cutlets. Heat 1 tbsp oil in a roasting tin at 220°C (210°C fan oven) Gas 7. Add lamb racks and roast, fat-side down, for 15 minutes, then turn and roast for a further 15–20 minutes; rest for 5 minutes. Drain off fat from tin, then stir in a splash of red wine and a cup of stock to make a jus. Wilt the rocket for 20 seconds in a covered pan, then toss with the garlic crisps. Mound on plates, add the lamb racks and drizzle with the pan jus.

# simple & satisfying

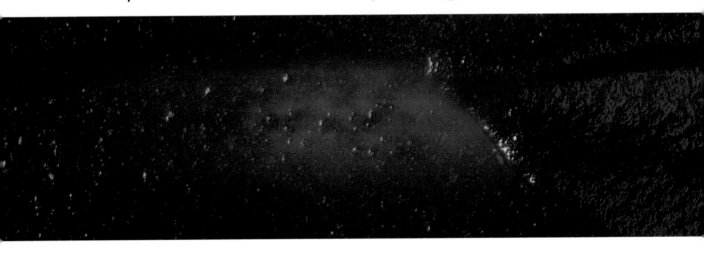

Chilled pumpkin & ginger soup

Wild mushroom & parsley broth

Celeriac & Parmesan soup

Braised lettuce with olive oil pomme purée

Seasonal vegetables in a herb nage

Herb-poached Jersey Royals with asparagus

Caramelised endive tart with walnut & roasted pear

Pan-fried gnocchi with tomato fondue & Parmesan

Roasted shallot & baby beetroot salad

Lasagne of wild mushrooms with garlic purée

Jerusalem artichoke mousse with peas

Spatzel topped with poached egg

Pumpkin & Parmesan risotto with queen scallops

Squid with crushed potatoes & saffron vinaigrette

Tea-smoked salmon with herb mayonnaise

Smoked bacon risotto with sweetcorn & Parmesan

Warm salad of duck breast & prunes with walnuts

Sautéed rabbit with rocket salad & carrot jus

Crispy pork belly with apple & frisée salad

# Chilled pumpkin & ginger soup

SERVES 6

*100g unsalted butter*

*900g peeled, deseeded*
  *pumpkin, roughly chopped*

*20g piece fresh root ginger, peeled*
  *and roughly sliced*

*70g sugar*

*salt and pepper*

*50ml dry white wine*

*1 litre chicken stock (page 156)*

*75ml double cream*

**crystallised ginger**

*40g piece fresh root ginger,*
  *peeled*

*2 tbsp icing sugar, plus a little*
  *extra to dust*

*oil, to deep-fry*

**pumpkin and ginger soup**    Melt the butter in a heavy-based saucepan. Add the chopped pumpkin, ginger, sugar and 1 tsp salt. Stir, then cover with a tight-fitting lid and sweat over a low heat for about 45 minutes, stirring occasionally. Remove the lid and continue cooking to reduce the liquid until the pumpkin is almost dry. Add the white wine and reduce by two-thirds, then add the chicken stock and cream and cook for 10 minutes. Cool slightly, then whiz the soup in a blender until smooth. Pass through a fine sieve into a bowl and leave to cool. Cover and chill.

**crystallised ginger**    Cut the ginger into julienne (or fine matchstick strips) and place in a bowl. Add the icing sugar, toss to coat and allow to stand for 45 minutes, turning from time to time. Tip the ginger into a strainer, rinse under cold running water to remove the sugar and dry thoroughly on kitchen paper. Heat a 4–5cm depth of oil in a small, deep, heavy pan to 150°C. Add the ginger julienne and deep-fry for 10 seconds, then remove immediately and drain on kitchen paper. Dust lightly with icing sugar.

**to serve**    Check the seasoning, then ladle the soup into chilled bowls and garnish with the crystallised ginger.

**note**    This fresh-tasting soup is also delicious served hot — simply warm through gently after puréeing and serve in warmed bowls, topped with the ginger garnish.

**as a canapé** Serve small portions of the soup – chilled or warm – in shot glasses. Halve the quantities for 8–10 canapé-sized portions. Omit the crystallised ginger garnish.

# Wild mushroom & parsley broth

SERVES 4

*2 tbsp unsalted butter*

*2 shallots, peeled and finely sliced*

*1/2 cup flat-leafed parsley leaves,*
  *stalks reserved*

*salt and pepper*

*1 litre chicken stock (page 156)*

*150g mixed wild mushrooms, such*
  *as chanterelles, girolles, ceps,*
  *shiitake, cleaned, trimmed, and*
  *sliced if large*

**soft-poached eggs**

*4 eggs*

*1 tbsp vinegar*

**parsley broth**   Put a wide, medium saucepan on a low heat and add 1 tbsp of the butter. When melted, add the shallots and reserved parsley stalks, and season with salt and pepper. Stir, then cover and sweat gently for 20 minutes, stirring occasionally. Add the chicken stock and bring to a simmer, then skim.

**mushrooms**   Heat a frying pan until very hot, then add the remaining butter and sauté the wild mushrooms for 2 minutes until lightly coloured all over. Add the mushrooms to the broth and simmer gently for 10 minutes, skimming as necessary. Add the parsley leaves and simmer for 6–8 minutes until they are tender. Check the seasoning.

**soft-poached eggs**   Cook these one at a time, while the broth is simmering. Two-thirds fill a deep pan with water, add the vinegar and bring to a simmer. Stir the water to create a circular movement, then slide in an egg and cook for about 1½–2 minutes until softly poached. Carefully lift out and refresh in a bowl of iced water. Repeat with the rest of the eggs.

**to serve**   When the broth is ready, take it off the heat. Immediately add the soft-poached eggs, using a slotted spoon to transfer them, and allow to warm through for 20 seconds. Ladle the soup into warmed bowls, placing a poached egg in the centre of each bowl. Serve straightaway.

**as a canapé**   This soup is a great way to appreciate the intense flavours of wild mushrooms and it can easily be down-sized to serve as an original canapé. Halve the quantities for 8 canapé-sized portions, Chop the parsley leaves and mushrooms, rather than leave them whole. Serve the soup in coffee cups, topped with a soft-poached quail egg to finish.

# Celeriac & Parmesan soup

SERVES 6

*250g celeriac, trimmed*

*75g unsalted butter*

*salt and pepper*

*100g Parmesan cheese, freshly
   grated, plus shavings to serve*

*750ml chicken stock (page 156)*

*250ml double cream*

*2 tbsp truffle oil, plus extra
   to drizzle*

**the soup base**    Peel and roughly dice the celeriac. Melt the butter in a medium pan over a low heat. Add the celeriac with a pinch of salt, stir, then cover and sweat for about 20 minutes until soft, stirring occasionally. Add the grated Parmesan and chicken stock and bring to a low simmer. Cook gently for 5 minutes.

**to enrich and purée**    Stir in the cream and truffle oil and simmer for a further 5 minutes. Allow to cool slightly, then whiz the soup in a blender until velvety smooth. Pass through a fine sieve into a clean pan or bowl.

**to serve**    Warm the soup gently, or allow to cool and chill if serving cold. Taste and adjust the seasoning, then serve. Top each portion with a drizzle of truffle oil and a few Parmesan shavings.

**variation**    Omit the Parmesan and truffle oil. Add 100g smoked haddock fillet when the stock has come to a simmer. Continue as above, enriching with cream and puréeing the soup as described. Serve hot.

# Braised lettuce with olive oil pomme purée

SERVES 4

**braised lettuce**

*8 baby Little Gem lettuce*

*50g unsalted butter*

*200g smoked bacon (optional),*
 *roughly chopped*

*1 onion, peeled and roughly*
 *chopped*

*1 carrot, peeled and roughly*
 *chopped*

*1 thyme sprig*

*300ml vegetable nage or chicken*
 *stock (page 156)*

**pomme purée**

*500g potatoes, such as Desirée or*
 *King Edward*

*salt and pepper*

*150ml olive oil*

*50g unsalted butter*

*100ml warm milk*

**braised lettuce**    Preheat the oven to 200°C (190°C fan oven) Gas 6. Remove any loose outer leaves from the lettuce. Heat a large ovenproof frying pan (or shallow flameproof casserole) over a high heat, then add the butter. When it is sizzling and just turning brown, add the lettuce and turn to colour on all sides; remove and set aside. Add the bacon to the pan, if using, and sauté for 2–3 minutes until coloured, then add the onion, carrot and thyme. Fry gently for about 5 minutes to soften, then return the lettuce to the pan. Pour in the nage or stock, cover with foil and braise in the oven for 12–15 minutes. Leave to stand for 10 minutes before serving.

**pomme purée**    Prepare this while the lettuce is braising. Peel the potatoes, cut into large, similar-sized pieces and place in a saucepan. Cover with cold water, add salt and bring to the boil. Lower the heat and simmer gently for 15–20 minutes until tender, drain. Push through a sieve or potato ricer into a clean saucepan. Place over a low heat and slowly beat in the olive oil and butter, then stir in the warm milk. Check the seasoning.

**to serve**    Spoon the pomme purée potato on to warmed plates, arrange the lettuce on top and drizzle with the cooking liquor.

**as a tart**    Follow the recipe for caramelised endive tart (page 76) using the braised lettuce in place of the endive, roasted baby shallots instead of pears, and walnuts rather than pine nuts. Serve drizzled with the pan juices.

**as a main course**    Braised lettuce with olive oil pomme purée is an excellent accompaniment to roasted pork fillet. Season 2 pork fillets (tenderloins) and quickly brown in a little oil in a frying pan over a high heat. Transfer to a roasting tin and cook in the oven at 200°C (190°C fan oven) Gas 6 for 15–20 minutes or until tender and cooked through. Rest for 5 minutes or so, then slice and serve with the braised lettuce and pomme purée.

# Seasonal vegetables in a herb nage

SERVES 4–6

### herb nage

3 onions

6 carrots

3 leeks, white part only

2 fennel bulbs

3 celery sticks

3 shallots

6 tarragon sprigs

6 parsley sprigs

1 tsp coriander seeds

12 black peppercorns

4 star anise

### spring/summer vegetables

120g podded peas

120g podded broad beans

150g sugar snap peas or
  mangetout

1 bunch of baby carrots (about 12),
  trimmed and scraped

12 baby turnips, trimmed

few young celery sticks or baby
  leeks, trimmed

### to finish

100g butter, chilled and diced

salt

squeeze of lemon juice

chopped parsley or chervil, or
  celery leaves

**herb nage**   Peel and roughly chop all the vegetables, place in a large stockpot or pan and add enough cold water to cover. Add the herbs and spices. Cover the surface with a piece of greaseproof paper and bring to the boil over a medium heat. Reduce the heat and simmer gently for about 20 minutes. Remove from the heat and allow to cool, then cover with cling film and leave to infuse in the fridge overnight.

**the next day**   Strain the nage through a fine sieve, discarding the vegetables and flavourings. Cover and keep in the fridge until ready to use.

**blanching the vegetables**   Bring a pan of salted water to the boil and cook the vegetables separately until al dente. Allow 3–4 minutes for peas and broad beans; 2–3 minutes for sugar snaps; 7–8 minutes for carrots and turnips; about 10 minutes for young celery sticks and baby leeks. Drain and immediately refresh each vegetable in iced water.

**to serve**   When ready to serve, pour 500ml nage into a medium saucepan and bring to the boil. Whisk in the butter, a piece at a time until emulsified. Season with salt and add lemon juice to taste. Add the blanched vegetables and warm through for 3–4 minutes. Serve in warmed bowls, finished with a sprinkling of chopped herbs or celery leaves.

## as an autumn or winter starter   Choose vegetables at their seasonal best. The illustrated combination works well: 120g swede; 4–6 small or medium parsnips; 4–6 medium carrots; 4–6 medium waxy potatoes such as La Ratte or Charlotte, scrubbed; 120g celery, trimmed. Peel the root vegetables, scrub the potatoes and halve the celery sticks. Cut the swede in half, then slice. Leave small parsnips whole; halve and core larger ones. Cook all vegetables separately in boiling water until al dente. Allow 15–20 minutes for the root vegetables and potatoes, depending on size; about 10 minutes for celery. Refresh in iced water and continue as above.

# Herb-poached Jersey Royals with asparagus

SERVES 4

*16–20 Jersey Royal new*
*  potatoes, scrubbed*
*1 litre vegetable nage (page 156)*
*1/2 garlic bulb (cut horizontally)*
*salt*
*1 medium bunch of chervil*
*1 small bunch each of thyme,*
*  parsley and tarragon*
*12 medium asparagus spears*
*50g unsalted butter, chilled and*
*  diced*
*Parmesan cheese shavings, to*
*  serve (optional)*

**herb-poached potatoes**    Put the Jersey Royals into a large saucepan with the nage, garlic and a pinch of salt; there must be enough liquid to cover the potatoes. Reserve half of the chervil and a little of each of the other herbs; tie the rest in a bundle with kitchen string and add to the pan. Bring to a gentle simmer, cover and cook for 12–15 minutes or until the potatoes are tender. Drain the potatoes and set aside, reserving 200ml of the cooking liquor. Bring this to the boil in a small pan and reduce by half; strain back into the large pan and set aside.

**the asparagus**    While the potatoes are cooking, trim the woody ends from the asparagus, then peel the lower end of the stalks. Blanch in a small, deep pan of boiling water (so the stalks cook in the water, while the tips steam gently) for about 3 minutes until just tender. Drain and refresh in iced water, then drain on kitchen paper.

**to serve**    Chop the reserved thyme, parsley and tarragon, and a little of the chervil. Whisk the butter into the reduced cooking liquor over a low heat. Add the potatoes, asparagus and chopped herbs, and gently warm through. Arrange the potatoes on warmed plates and top with the asparagus. Garnish with chervil and drizzle with the reduced cooking liquor. Scatter over the Parmesan shavings if using, and serve immediately.

**note**    This is a delicious way to serve Jersey Royals when they are in season; alternatively, use Nicola or Charlotte potatoes instead.

# Caramelised endive tart with walnut & roasted pear

*100g unsalted butter*

*2 large white Belgian endive (chicory), halved lengthways*

*salt and pepper*

*200ml chicken stock (page 156)*

*100g shelled walnuts*

*4 ripe Comice or Williams' pears*

*1 tbsp sugar*

*squeeze of lemon juice*

*250g ready-made puff pastry (thawed if frozen)*

**caramelised endive**    Place a large frying pan over a medium heat, then add 75g of the butter. Season both sides of the endive halves, then place cut-side down in the pan. Cook for 6–7 minutes until golden brown, then flip over and cook for a further 2 minutes. Drain off excess butter from the pan, then add the chicken stock and simmer for about 6–7 minutes until the endive is cooked and the liquor is reduced to a glaze. Check the seasoning and allow to cool.

**toasted walnuts**    Preheat the oven to 210°C (200°C fan oven) Gas 6. Scatter the walnuts on a baking tray and toast in the oven for 5–6 minutes. Season with salt and set aside to cool. When cool, roughly chop the nuts.

**pan-roasted pears**    Peel, core and roughly chop or slice the pears. Place a large frying pan over a medium heat and add the remaining butter. When foaming, add the pears and cook, stirring occasionally, for 4–5 minutes until evenly coloured on all sides. Tip out half of the butter, then return the pan to the heat. Add the sugar and stir for 30 seconds or so until it dissolves. Stir in 2 tbsp water to deglaze. Finish with a squeeze of lemon juice.

**assembling the tarts**    Roll out the puff pastry to a rectangle, 5mm thick, then cut 4 rectangles, about 2cm larger all round than the cut endive. Prick the pastry all over with a fork. Lay an endive half, cut-side uppermost, on each puff pastry rectangle, making sure it is centred, and press gently into the pastry; save any endive pan juices. Bake the tarts in the oven for 15–17 minutes, until the pastry is golden brown and risen around the edges.

**to serve**    Place each endive tart on a warmed plate, spoon over the pan-roasted pear mix and sprinkle with the chopped walnuts. Drizzle over any reserved pan juices and serve warm.

**as a main course** Omit the pastry.
Halve 2 poussins lengthways, season and pan-fry,
skin-side down, in a little hot butter for about
5 minutes until deep golden. Turn and cook on the
other side for a minute or two, then roast in the
oven at 200°C (190°C fan oven) Gas 6 for about
15 minutes. Rest for 10 minutes, then serve with the
caramelised endive, roasted pears, walnuts and pan
juices. The flavour combination works brilliantly.

**as a canapé** Shape the gnocchi mixture into a slightly thinner roll. Once cooked, cut into 2–3cm discs and pan-fry until golden brown, as described. Place on a tray and top each one with a little tomato fondue and a sliver of Parmesan. Serve warm, as an elegant canapé.

# Pan-fried gnocchi with tomato fondue & Parmesan

SERVES 4–6

**gnocchi**

*3 large baking potatoes, such as*
*   Desirée or King Edward, about*
*   800g in total*
*125g plain flour, sifted*
*125g Parmesan cheese, freshly*
*   grated*
*1 whole egg, plus 2 egg yolks*
*3 tbsp finely chopped chives*
*salt*

**tomato fondue**

*5 large plum tomatoes*
*1 small bunch of thyme sprigs*
*1 small bunch of rosemary sprigs*
*4 tbsp olive oil*
*1/2 onion, peeled and finely diced*
*2 garlic cloves, peeled and cracked*
*salt and pepper*

**to assemble**

*30g plain flour, to dust*
*60g unsalted butter*
*50g Parmesan cheese, shaved*
*handful of rocket leaves, tossed in*
*   a little vinaigrette (page 157)*

**gnocchi**  Preheat the oven to 200°C (190°C fan oven) Gas 6. Prick the potato skins, then put the potatoes on a baking tray and bake for about 1 hour until tender. Leave to cool, then halve and scoop out the flesh. Pass this through a potato ricer or a medium sieve into a bowl. Add the flour, Parmesan, egg, egg yolks and chives. Mix thoroughly, using an electric mixer and season with salt to taste. Lay a large sheet of all-purpose cling film on a work surface. Spoon a 15–20cm length of gnocchi mixture along the front edge, leaving a good length of cling film free at both ends. Roll the mixture tightly in the cling film, then twist and tie the ends to secure. Repeat with the rest of the mixture. Bring a large pan of water to the boil and cook the gnocchi rolls in the boiling water for 10 minutes. Remove with a slotted spoon and refresh in iced water.

**tomato fondue**  Make a small cross incision on the base of each tomato, immerse in boiling water for 5 seconds, then remove and refresh in iced water. Peel away the skins and roughly chop the tomatoes. Tie the herb sprigs together in muslin or with string. Put a medium saucepan over a low heat and pour in the olive oil. Add the onion, garlic, herbs and a pinch of salt. Cover and sweat for about 10 minutes until the onion is soft, then add the chopped tomatoes. Gently simmer for 20 minutes, stirring occasionally, until the tomato fondue is well reduced, thick and pulpy. Check the seasoning, remove the garlic and set aside.

**to assemble**  Unwrap the cooked gnocchi, cut into 2cm lengths and dust with flour. Heat a non-stick frying pan over a medium heat. Add the butter and heat until melted and light brown, then add the gnocchi and cook, turning occasionally, for 3–5 minutes until golden brown. In the meantime, warm the tomato fondue in the microwave, or a small pan over low heat. Drain the gnocchi on kitchen paper and arrange on warmed plates. Spoon the tomato fondue alongside and top with Parmesan shavings and rocket leaves. Serve at once.

**note**  Prepared in this way, the gnocchi rolls can be made ahead and kept wrapped in cling film in the fridge for up to 3 days; they can also be frozen. If you prefer not to use cling film, simply roll the gnocchi mixture into small balls in the palm of your hand and drop straight into the boiling water, then continue as above.

# Roasted shallot & baby beetroot salad

SERVES 4

*2 banana shallots (see note)*
*2 tbsp unsalted butter*
*300g girolles or other wild*
  *mushrooms, cleaned*
*50ml white wine vinegar*
*50ml sweet white wine*
*2 tsp chopped parsley*
*salt and pepper*
*2 bunches of baby beetroot*
  *(see note)*
*300ml vegetable stock*
*1 tsp sugar*
*½ onion, peeled and roughly*
  *diced*
*1 garlic clove, peeled*
*2 tbsp olive oil*
*150g salad leaves, such as baby*
  *beetroot leaves, baby chard*
  *and wild rocket*
*1 tbsp aged balsamic vinegar*

**roasted shallots**   Preheat the oven to 175°C (165°C fan oven) Gas 3. Prick the shallots all over with a cocktail stick, but don't peel them. Place on a baking tray and roast until soft, 30–40 minutes depending on size.

**pickled girolles**   Heat a medium frying pan and add 1 tbsp unsalted butter. When melted, add a third of the mushrooms and sauté until lightly coloured. Add the wine vinegar and reduce until almost dry.  Add the wine and reduce until the mushrooms are coated with a glaze. Add the chopped parsley, season to taste, then tip on to a plate to cool.

**poached beetroot**   Pick off any leaves from the beetroot that are suitable for the salad; wash and reserve. Trim the beetroot tops, leaving on a tuft of the leafy stalks, then peel. Put them into a small saucepan with 200ml of the vegetable stock, the sugar, a pinch of salt and a few twists of black pepper. Bring to a simmer and cook for about 20 minutes until the beetroot are tender. Leave them to cool in the reduced cooking juices.

**wild mushroom purée**   Heat a small saucepan and add 1 tbsp unsalted butter. When melted, add the onion and garlic with a pinch of salt. Cover and sweat over a low heat for 15–20 minutes until very soft. Meanwhile, place a large frying pan on a high heat and add 1 tbsp olive oil. Add the remaining 200g mushrooms, season with salt and sauté for 3–4 minutes until just turning golden; remove and drain on kitchen paper. Now tip the mushrooms on to the softened onion, along with 100ml vegetable stock, and simmer for 3 minutes. Discard the garlic, cool slightly, then whiz in a blender until smooth. Transfer to a bowl, check seasoning and set aside.

**to serve**   Halve the roasted shallots lengthways. Warm through in the oven or microwave along with the mushroom purée, if necessary. Dress the salad leaves with 1 tbsp olive oil, balsamic vinegar and seasoning. Place the shallot halves on warmed plates and top with the warm mushroom purée; pile the salad at one end. Arrange the baby beetroot and pickled girolles alongside and drizzle with a little of the beetroot liquor.

**note**   If banana shallots are not available, use 12 large, regular shallots instead. Similarly, if you cannot find baby beetroot, substitute 2 standard beetroot; peel and cut into large dice before poaching.

# Lasagne of wild mushrooms with garlic purée

SERVES 4

### shallot stock

2 tbsp unsalted butter

3 shallots, peeled and finely
    chopped

2 garlic cloves, peeled

5 thyme sprigs

500ml vegetable nage or chicken
    stock (page 156)

### garlic purée

3 garlic bulbs, separated into cloves
    and peeled

200ml double cream

salt and pepper

a little milk (if needed)

### creamed mushrooms

300g mixed wild mushrooms, such
    as chanterelles, girolles, ceps,
    shiitake, cleaned and trimmed

1 tbsp olive oil

60g unsalted butter, chilled and
    diced

2 garlic cloves, peeled and cracked

1 small bunch of chervil

1 tbsp chopped thyme

1 tbsp chopped parsley

### lasagne

150g fresh pasta sheets, 2mm thick
    (page 157), or 8 wonton wrappers

**shallot stock**    Heat 1 tbsp butter in a pan over a low heat, add the shallots, garlic and thyme, then cover and sweat gently for 5–7 minutes until soft, but not coloured. Add the nage or stock and simmer for 15 minutes. Take off the heat and leave to infuse for 15 minutes. Discard the garlic and thyme; measure 200ml stock. (Any remaining shallot stock can be frozen.)

**garlic purée**    Put the garlic into a small pan, cover with cold water and bring to the boil. Drain, and repeat this process three times. Return the garlic to the pan, add the cream with a pinch of salt and bring to a low simmer. Cook gently, stirring occasionally, for about 15 minutes until the garlic is soft and the cream is reduced. Tip into a blender and whiz until smooth, then pass through a fine sieve into a bowl; check the seasoning and keep warm.

**creamed mushrooms**    Quarter or slice any larger mushrooms. Heat the olive oil in a large frying pan over a high heat. Add a third of the butter and once it starts foaming, add the garlic and mushrooms and season with salt and pepper. Sauté for 3–4 minutes until the mushrooms are tender, then add the shallot stock and reduce by two-thirds. Meanwhile, set aside a few chervil sprigs for garnish; chop the rest of the leaves, discarding the stems. Remove the garlic from the mushrooms. Stir in the remaining butter to emulsify, add the chopped herbs, check the seasoning and keep warm.

**to serve**    Reheat the garlic purée gently in a small pan; it should be a pouring consistency, thin with a little milk if it is too thick. If using pasta, cut into eight 10cm squares. Add the pasta or wonton wrappers to a pan of boiling salted water and cook until al dente, about 1–1½ minutes; drain well. Layer the lasagne on warmed plates, starting with a layer of creamed mushrooms, then a dab of garlic purée, then a square of pasta or a wonton wrapper. Repeat these layers and finish with a layer of mushrooms. Garnish with chervil sprigs and serve.

**as a main course**    Lightly poach 2 boneless chicken breasts in chicken stock for 15–20 minutes until tender; rest for a few minutes. Cook 100g spinach leaves in a covered pan with 1 tbsp water for 30 seconds – 1 minute until just wilted; drain well, then chop. Slice the chicken and add to the creamed mushrooms with the chopped spinach. Layer the lasagne as above.

# Jerusalem artichoke mousse with peas

SERVES 6

*700g Jerusalem artichokes*
*salt and pepper*
*juice of 1/2 lemon*
*1 whole egg, plus 2 egg yolks*
*150ml double cream*

**to assemble**
*2 tsp softened butter*
*150g shelled peas*
*Jerusalem artichoke crisps*
*(page 13), to garnish (optional)*

**Jerusalem artichoke purée** Peel the artichokes and immediately place in a pan of cold salted water with the lemon juice added to prevent discolouration. Bring to the boil, lower the heat and simmer for 15–20 minutes until tender. Drain, then whiz the artichokes in a blender to a purée. Transfer to a medium saucepan and bring to a simmer. Cook over a low heat until the artichoke purée is reduced by half and thickened. Set aside to cool. When cool, beat in the egg, egg yolks and cream. Season with salt and pepper to taste.

**baking the soufflés** Preheat the oven to 160°C (150°C fan oven) Gas 2 1/2. Grease 6 individual 200–250ml soufflé dishes generously with a teaspoon of softened butter. Spoon the artichoke mousse into the dishes to two-thirds them. Stand in a shallow roasting tin and surround with warm water to come halfway up the sides of the dishes. Bake for 40–50 minutes until the mousses are lightly firm to the touch.

**cooking the peas** About 10 minutes before the mousses will be ready, add the peas to a pan of boiling salted water. Simmer for 3 minutes or until just tender; drain.

**to serve** Place the soufflé dishes on warmed plates and spoon the peas on top of the mousses. Serve artichoke crisps as an extra garnish if you like.

**as a main course** Season a 1.5kg oven-ready free-range chicken with salt and pepper, and poach whole in a well-seasoned nage or chicken stock with a handful of tarragon sprigs for 40–50 minutes until tender and cooked through. Line the base of the soufflé dishes with baking parchment before greasing. Once cooked, run a knife around the mousses and turn out on to warmed large plates. Carve the chicken and serve with the mousses.

# Spatzel topped with poached egg

SERVES 4

**spatzel**
*75g unsalted butter*
*250g plain flour*
*1 tsp salt*
*½ tsp freshly grated nutmeg*
*2 whole eggs, plus 3 egg yolks*
*140ml milk*
*dash of vegetable oil*

**soft-poached eggs**
*dash of vinegar*
*4 eggs*

**to finish**
*75g unsalted butter*
*50ml hazelnut oil*
*salt and pepper*

**the spatzel mixture**    Melt the butter in a small saucepan over a medium heat and cook until light golden brown, then remove from the heat. Combine the flour, salt and nutmeg in a large bowl and make a well in the middle. In a separate bowl, whisk the eggs and egg yolks with the warm butter and milk, then slowly pour into the flour well. Gradually draw in the flour from the sides of the well with your fingers and mix to a soft dough. Cover and leave to rest in the fridge for 30 minutes.

**to cook the spatzel**    Bring a large pan of salted water to the boil. Spread the dough on a chopping board or flat tray to an even 3mm thickness. You will need to cook the spatzel in several batches. Hold the edge of the board or tray partly over the pan of boiling water. Using a palette knife held at a 20° angle, cut off thin strips of dough and knock them into the water, about 15 or 20 at a time. (Alternatively, push the dough through a slotted spatzel plate or colander directly into the water.) Cook for about 1 minute. Using a slotted spoon, lift out the cooked noodles and put into a bowl of iced water to cool, then remove and drain. Place on a tray lined with kitchen paper to dry. Continue cooking in batches until the dough is used up. When finished, toss the noodles in a little oil to prevent them from sticking. Reserve in the fridge.

**soft-poached eggs**    Half-fill a large, shallow pan with water, add the vinegar and bring to a simmer. Stir the water to create a circular movement, then poach the eggs for about 1½–2 minutes until softly set. Carefully remove and drain on kitchen paper; keep warm in a low oven.

**to finish**    While the eggs are poaching, place a sauté pan over a medium heat, add the butter and cook until lightly browned. Immediately add the spatzel and sauté for 2 minutes. Drizzle in the hazelnut oil, check the seasoning and divide among warmed plates. Top with the poached eggs and flick a pinch of salt on top of each egg to serve.

# Pumpkin & Parmesan risotto with queen scallops

SERVES 6

**pumpkin stock**

*40g unsalted butter*

*300g peeled, deseeded pumpkin,
  roughly chopped*

*50g Parmesan cheese, roughly
  chopped*

*100ml medium dry white wine*

*750ml vegetable nage (page 156)*

*2 tbsp double cream*

**risotto**

*40g unsalted butter*

*½ onion, peeled and finely diced*

*300g arborio or other risotto rice*

*salt and pepper*

*250g shelled queen scallops*

*2 tbsp olive oil*

*squeeze of lemon juice*

*2 tbsp finely chopped chives*

*20g Parmesan cheese, freshly
  grated, plus shavings to garnish*

**pumpkin and Parmesan stock**    Melt the butter in a large saucepan. Add the pumpkin and chopped Parmesan, cover and sweat over a low heat, stirring occasionally until soft and watery, about 30 minutes. Remove the lid and simmer until the water is totally reduced, then add the white wine and reduce by two-thirds. Add the stock and cream and simmer for 8–10 minutes. Cool slightly, then whiz in a blender until smooth. Return to the pan and bring to a simmer.

**the risotto**    Heat 20g butter in a medium non-stick saucepan. Add the onion, cover and sweat for 7–8 minutes until soft. Add the rice and stir over the heat for 2 minutes until the grains are translucent. Add the pumpkin stock, a small ladleful at a time, stirring constantly and waiting for each addition to be absorbed before adding the next. This process should take 15–20 minutes; the risotto is ready when the rice is al dente and the texture is creamy (you may not need all of the stock). Check the seasoning and finish with the remaining knob of butter.

**pan-frying the scallops**    Pat the scallops dry with kitchen paper, then season lightly with salt. Heat a large frying pan over a high heat, then add 2 tbsp olive oil. Sauté the scallops in the hot oil for 30–45 seconds until they just start to colour at the edges, then remove and drain on kitchen paper. Squeeze a little lemon juice over them.

**to serve**    Stir the chopped chives and grated Parmesan through the risotto. Spoon into warmed bowls and top with the sautéed scallops. Scatter Parmesan shavings over the scallops and serve immediately.

**as a main course** Increase the variety and quantity of shellfish. Try pan-roasted scallops, prawns and cracked crab claws. Or cook 500g each fresh mussels and cockles or small clams in a tightly covered pan with 150ml dry white wine and ½ finely sliced shallot for 3–4 minutes until the shells open; discard any that remain closed. Drain and serve on top of the risotto.

# Squid with crushed potatoes & saffron vinaigrette

SERVES 4

16–24 baby squid (4–6 per person
   depending on size, see note),
   cleaned
400g new potatoes
salt and pepper
50g unsalted butter
1 tbsp chopped parsley
1 tbsp chopped chives or dill
2 tbsp olive oil
juice of 1/2 lemon, or to taste

saffron vinaigrette
20ml white wine vinegar
large pinch of saffron threads
4 tbsp olive oil

**saffron vinaigrette**   Make this first. Put the wine vinegar into a small saucepan with 1 tsp water and the saffron threads. Bring to the boil over a medium heat, then immediately take off the heat and set aside to infuse for 2 hours.

**preparing the squid**   Rinse the whole baby squid pouches and separate tentacles, pat dry with kitchen paper and set aside.

**crushed potatoes**   Put the potatoes into a pan, cover with cold water, add salt and bring to the boil. Lower the heat and simmer for 12–15 minutes until just tender. Drain the potatoes and peel while still warm, using a small knife. Return to the pan and crush the potatoes lightly, with a fork. Add the butter and chopped herbs, and fork through. Season with salt and pepper to taste; keep warm.

**pan-frying the squid**   Heat a large non-stick frying pan over a high heat, then add the 2 tbsp olive oil. When it is hot and almost on the point of smoking, add the squid and season with salt. Sauté for 1–1 1/2 minutes or until the squid are lightly coloured and just cooked through. Add a generous squeeze of lemon juice and take off the heat.

**to serve**   To finish the vinaigrette, stir in the 4 tbsp olive oil and a pinch of salt. Put a small mound of crushed potatoes in the centre of each warmed serving plate. Arrange the squid on top and dress with the saffron vinaigrette. Serve immediately.

**note**   If baby squid are unavailable, use cleaned, full-sized squid; you will need 500g prepared weight. Slice the body pouches into rings and cut the tentacles into smaller pieces if necessary.

**as a main course**   Serve each portion with a pan-fried fillet of red mullet, sea bass or bream – the flavours complement each other perfectly. Buy 4 fish fillets, each about 125g. Before you cook the squid, pan-fry them, skin-side down, in a little hot butter and oil for 1 1/2–2 minutes, then flip over and cook for a further 30 seconds or so. Leave to rest in a warm place while you cook the squid.

# Tea-smoked salmon with herb mayonnaise

*Illustrated on page 90*

SERVES 4

**tea-smoked salmon**

*500g salmon fillet, trimmed and*
*    skinned*

*4 tbsp olive oil*

*salt and pepper*

*40g Lapsang Souchong Tea*

**herb mayonnaise**

*3 egg yolks*

*juice of 1/2 lemon*

*200ml olive oil*

*300ml grapeseed oil*

*10 tbsp chopped soft-leafed herbs,*
*    such as parsley, basil, tarragon,*
*    chervil and dill*

**to serve**

*150g baby salad leaves, such as*
*    spinach, chard or rocket leaves*

*dash of extra virgin olive oil*

*a little red wine vinegar*

*8 small thin rounds of rye or*
*    multigrain bread, lightly toasted*

**herb mayonnaise**    Prepare this in advance. Put the egg yolks, lemon juice and 1 tsp salt into a bowl and whisk together until smooth. Combine the olive and grapeseed oils in a jug. Slowly add the blended oils to the yolk mixture, drop by drop to begin with, then in a steady drizzle, whisking constantly with a hand-held electric whisk to create an emulsion. (If the mixture splits, add 1 tsp of boiling water to one side of the bowl and whisk to re-emulsify.) Taste and adjust the seasoning. Finally, fold in the chopped herbs. This herb mayonnaise can be kept for up to 3 days in the fridge.

**tea-smoked salmon**    Use a large, deep pan (not your best one) or a wok with a tight-fitting lid. Check over the salmon for pin bones and remove any with tweezers. Take a large sheet of foil and fold into 3 or 4 layers until it is just bigger than the salmon. Pierce the foil several times with a thin skewer and rub with a little oil. Season both sides of the salmon with salt and pepper, then lay on the foil. Put the dry pan or wok over a high heat. When it is very hot, add the tea and stir with a spoon for 5–10 seconds to toast. Lay the foil holding the fish directly on top of the tea. Cover tightly with the lid and smoke the fish for at least 5 minutes or up to 8 minutes for thick fillets. Lift out the salmon on the foil and brush with a little olive oil, then wrap in the foil and leave to rest for 5 minutes or so.

**to serve**    Dress the salad leaves with a dash of olive oil, a little red wine vinegar and salt to taste. Flake the warm salmon. Place 2 toast rounds on each warmed serving plate. Top each with a generous spoonful of herb mayonnaise and arrange the salmon flakes on top. Finish with the salad leaves and serve.

## tea-smoked haddock as a main course    *Illustrated on page 91*

Hot-smoke 4 skinned haddock fillet portions, about 170g each, as above, allowing an extra 3 minutes. Serve topped with a soft-poached egg (see page 85) and accompanied by the salad and herb mayonnaise.

Or simply hot-smoke 4 larger salmon fillet portions, about 170g each, and serve with the herb mayonnaise and salad, or asparagus tagliatelle (page 129).

# Smoked bacon risotto with sweetcorn & Parmesan

SERVES 4

### bacon stock

*2 tbsp unsalted butter*

*1 large onion, peeled and roughly chopped*

*2 garlic cloves, peeled*

*3 thyme sprigs*

*3 bay leaves*

*350g smoked bacon, derinded and roughly chopped*

*1 litre chicken stock (page 156)*

### sweetcorn

*1 corn-on-the-cob, outer husk removed*

### risotto

*80g unsalted butter*

*60g smoked bacon, derinded and diced*

*200g arborio or other risotto rice*

*½ medium onion, finely diced*

*2 tbsp double cream*

*salt and pepper*

*75g Parmesan cheese, freshly grated, to serve*

**bacon stock**  Melt 1 tbsp butter in a medium saucepan. Add the onion, garlic, thyme and bay leaves. Stir, then cover and sweat over a low heat for about 10 minutes or until the onion softens. In the meantime, melt the remaining butter in a large frying pan, add the chopped bacon and sauté until golden brown. Add the bacon to the onion, pour in the stock and bring to a simmer. Continue to simmer for 20 minutes. Skim off any fat that rises to the surface, then strain the stock into a clean pan. Check the seasoning; if the stock tastes too salty, dilute it with a little water.

**sweetcorn**  While the stock is simmering, cook the corn-on-the-cob in boiling water for 20–25 minutes until the kernels are tender; don't add salt during cooking as it will toughen the corn. Drain, and when cool enough to handle, hold the cob upright and shave off the kernels carefully, using a sharp knife. Set aside; keep warm.

**risotto**  Heat 1 tbsp of the butter in a frying pan, add the diced bacon and sauté over a medium heat until lightly coloured. Drain on kitchen paper and set aside. Heat 40g butter in a medium non-stick saucepan. Add the diced onion, cover and sweat over a low heat for 8–10 minutes until soft. In the meantime, bring the bacon stock back to a simmer. Add the rice and sautéed bacon to the onion and stir over the heat for 2 minutes. Start to add the stock in small ladlefuls, waiting for each addition to be absorbed before adding the next and stirring constantly. Continue adding the stock in this way until the risotto is creamy and the rice is al dente; it will take 15–20 minutes (you may not need all of the stock). Finish with the cream and a knob of butter. Check the seasoning.

**to serve**  Spoon the risotto on to warmed plates, scatter the sweetcorn on top and finish with grated Parmesan.

# Warm salad of duck breast & prunes with walnuts

SERVES 4

*50g shelled walnuts*

*salt and pepper*

*2 boneless duck breasts, with skin,*
*each about 180g*

*1 tbsp vegetable oil*

*2 tbsp unsalted butter*

**tea-infused prunes**

*2 English breakfast tea bags*

*finely pared zest and juice of*
*1 orange*

*2 cinnamon sticks*

*1 tbsp sugar*

*16 semi-dried Agen prunes*

**spinach salad**

*150g baby spinach leaves*

*1 tbsp olive oil*

*squeeze of lemon juice*

**tea-infused prunes**    Prepare these in advance. Put the tea bags and 500ml water into a pan with the orange zest, orange juice, cinnamon sticks and sugar. Slowly bring to the boil, then add the prunes and simmer for 5 minutes. Take of the heat and allow the prunes to cool in the liquor. Leave to steep for at least 2 hours, but preferably overnight.

**walnuts**    Preheat the oven to 210°C (200°C fan oven) Gas 6. Scatter the walnuts on a baking tray and toast in the oven for 6 minutes. Season the hot nuts with salt, then leave to cool. Break the nuts into smaller pieces.

**pan-frying the duck breasts**    Using a sharp knife, score the skin side of the duck breasts on the diagonal and again crossways to give a diamond pattern on the skin. Season both sides of the duck breasts generously with salt and pepper. Place a non-stick frying pan over a medium heat and add the vegetable oil. Put the duck breasts in the pan, skin-side down, and cook for 5 minutes until golden. Flip over and add 1 tbsp butter to the pan. Cook for a further 4–5 minutes for medium rare; 6–7 minutes for medium; or 10 minutes for well done. Remove the duck breasts from the pan and leave to rest in a warm place for 10 minutes.

**spinach salad**    Shred the spinach leaves and dress with a dash of olive oil and a squeeze of lemon juice. Season with salt and pepper.

**to serve**    Drain the prunes, reserving 5–6 tbsp of the liquor; discard the cinnamon and orange zest. Put the prunes and reserved liquor into a small saucepan and heat gently for a few minutes. Lift out the prunes and keep warm. Bring the liquor back to the boil, then reduce the heat and whisk in the remaining 1 tbsp butter to create an emulsion. Slice the duck breasts across the grain into thin slices. Arrange on warmed plates with the prunes and dressed spinach. Drizzle the duck with the tea-butter emulsion and scatter the toasted walnuts over the salad.

**as a main course** Pan-fry 4 duck breasts rather than two, and make a swede and potato gratin (page 108) to serve as an accompaniment. Cook the spinach leaves in a covered pan with a dash of water until just wilted, then drain. Place the whole duck breasts on warm plates with the wilted spinach, tea-infused prunes and a portion of gratin. Top with the whole toasted walnuts to serve.

# Sautéed rabbit with rocket salad & carrot jus

SERVES 4

*2 saddles of rabbit, about 400g
  each, filleted and trimmed
  (see note)*

*salt and pepper*

*1 tbsp unsalted butter*

**carrot jus**

*300ml fresh carrot juice (see note)*

*juice of 1/2 lemon*

*pinch of sugar*

*1 tbsp double cream*

*15g unsalted butter, chilled and
  diced*

*2 tbsp tarragon leaves, finely
  chopped*

**rocket salad**

*150g rocket leaves, trimmed*

*1 tbsp olive oil*

*1 tbsp balsamic vinegar*

**carrot jus**  Prepare this first. Pour the carrot juice into a small saucepan and add the lemon juice, sugar, cream and a pinch of salt. Bring to the boil, then simmer to reduce by two-thirds. Whisk in the cold butter to emulsify. Taste and adjust the seasoning; keep warm.

**pan-frying the rabbit**  Season the rabbit fillets with salt. Heat a heavy-based frying pan over a medium heat, then add the butter. When melted and sizzling, add the rabbit fillets and sauté for 5–6 minutes or until golden and cooked through. Transfer to a warm plate, cover loosely with foil and set aside to rest 5–6 minutes.

**rocket salad**  Dress the rocket leaves with the olive oil and balsamic vinegar, seasoning with salt and pepper to taste.

**to serve**  Bring the carrot jus back to a simmer. Slice each rabbit fillet lengthways into 3 slices. Arrange them in the centre of warmed plates with the dressed rocket. Stir the tarragon into the carrot jus and spoon generously around the rabbit slices. Serve immediately.

**note**  Ask your butcher to bone the rabbit saddles; you should end up with 4 neat fillets. If you have an electric juicer, make your own carrot juice and pass it through a fine sieve; otherwise you can buy fresh carrot juice.

**as a main course**  Ask your butcher to bone out the hind legs of the 2 rabbits. Lay each flat on a buttered piece of foil. Season and sprinkle with a little chopped tarragon. Roll into a sausage shape, wrap in the foil and roast at 220°C (210°C fan oven) Gas 7 for about 15 minutes. Check that the rabbit is cooked through by inserting a small knife into the thickest part. Let rest for 5 minutes or so, then serve with the sautéed rabbit, salad and carrot jus.

# Crispy pork belly with apple & frisée salad

**SERVES 6**

*800g pork belly (ideally in one piece)*

*1 litre chicken stock (page 156)*

*15g thyme sprigs*

*salt*

**mirepoix**

*2 bay leaves*

*3 garlic cloves, peeled*

*1 carrot, peeled and roughly chopped*

*1 onion, peeled and roughly chopped*

*1 celery stick, roughly chopped*

**apple and frisée salad**

*200g frisée (pale leaves only)*

*1 Granny Smith apple*

*1 tbsp olive oil*

*1 tbsp aged balsamic vinegar*

*salt and pepper*

**to finish**

*20g unsalted butter*

*few rosemary sprigs*

*2 tbsp aged balsamic vinegar*

**preparing the pork**    Soak the pork belly overnight in plenty of cold water. The next day, drain the pork and put into a cooking pot or pan (large enough to accommodate it with cooking liquid). Add 1 litre cold water and bring to the boil rapidly to blanch the pork. Pour off the water, then add the chicken stock, thyme and 1 tsp salt. Add the mirepoix ingredients and bring to a low simmer. Skim, then cook at a low simmer for 3 hours, skimming the surface from time to time. If necessary, top up the cooking liquor with water during cooking to ensure the pork stays covered. Remove from the heat and leave the pork belly to cool in the cooking liquid.

**pressing the pork**    When cool, take the pork belly out of the pan. Remove the skin and any bones, then lay the pork belly flat on a tray, or in a casserole large enough to take it flat. Cover the pork with another tray, or container that fits inside the casserole, and press as hard as possible. Uncover, then wrap the pork tightly in cling film and press between the trays (or containers) as before. Place in the fridge, weigh down with heavy objects and leave overnight.

**apple and frisée salad**    Prepare this just before serving. Tear the pale frisée leaves into small pieces. Peel, core and slice the apple into julienne and place in a bowl with the frisée. Drizzle with the olive oil and balsamic vinegar and toss to mix. Season with salt and pepper to taste.

**to assemble**    Unwrap the pork belly and cut into 2cm thick slices, using a sharp knife. Season with salt. Heat the butter in a non-stick frying pan over a medium heat. Fry the pork belly in batches, with a few sprigs of rosemary, until golden and crisp. Drain the pork on kitchen paper, then arrange on plates with the salad. Add the balsamic vinegar to the pan juices, stir to deglaze, then drizzle over the salad and around the plate.

**as a main course**    This dish works exceptionally well as a winter main course – real comfort food. Simply double up the quantities, cut the pressed pork into large wedges, pan-fry and serve with the apple salad and rich, buttery mashed potato.

**as a canapé**    Cut the pork into bite-sized chunks, pan-fry as above until crisp, then skewer on to wooden cocktail sticks and serve on a bed of apple and frisée salad.

# food for groups

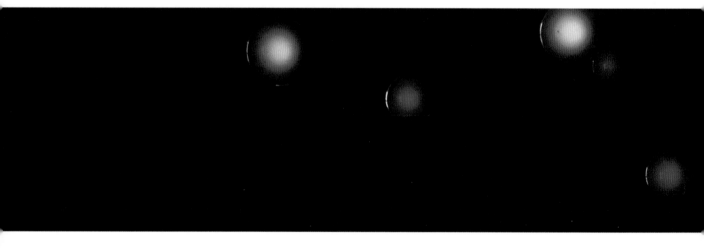

Ragout of borlotti beans & baby onions

Gazpacho consommé with scallop ravioli

Caramelised onion and mushroom tarts

Swede & potato gratin with pine nuts

Terrine of herb-cooked leeks & crab salad

Anchovy & tomato terrine with basil purée

Blinis topped with curried oysters

Creamed salt cod & celeriac soup

Crab croquettes with tomato dipping sauce

Home-cured salmon with grainy mustard dressing

Honey glazed ham with celeriac rémoulade

Oxtail & lentil ragout with root vegetables

Beef bourguignonne tartlets

Roasted lamb cannelloni with minted peas

# Ragout of borlotti beans & baby onions

SERVES 6

*175g dried borlotti, haricot or*
*flageolet beans (or a mixture),*
*soaked in cold water overnight*
*1 onion, peeled and quartered*
*1 carrot, peeled and quartered*
*1 celery stick, trimmed and*
*quartered*
*3 garlic cloves, peeled*
*5–6 thyme sprigs*
*100g piece smoked bacon, cut into*
*large pieces*
*2 litres chicken stock (page 156)*
*20 baby onions*
*75g chilled unsalted butter, in*
*pieces*
*salt and pepper*
*lemon juice, to taste*
*5–6 tarragon sprigs, leaves*
*stripped and chopped*

**to cook the beans**    Drain the pre-soaked beans, put them into a large saucepan and cover with fresh cold water. Bring to the boil, then drain and return the beans to the pan. Add the onion, carrot, celery, garlic, thyme and bacon. Pour in the stock, bring to a gentle boil and cook, stirring occasionally, until the beans are tender, 1½–2 hours or longer. Remove from the heat and leave the beans to cool in the liquor for about 15 minutes. Strain the liquor into a large pan and reserve; set the beans aside.

**to cook the baby onions**    Immerse the onions in hot water for 30 seconds to loosen the skins, then peel. Return the reserved cooking liquor (from the beans) to the heat, add the peeled baby onions and simmer about 10–12 minutes until tender. Remove the onions with a slotted spoon and set aside.

**to finish**    Bring the liquor back to the boil and boil to reduce by half. In the meantime, remove the bacon, vegetables, garlic and thyme from the beans and discard. Whisk the cold butter into the reduced cooking liquor, a piece at a time, to emulsify the sauce. Add the beans and baby onions and simmer for a few minutes to warm through – the ragout should have a thick, soup-like consistency.

**to serve**    Season with salt and pepper and add a squeeze of lemon juice to taste. Stir in the chopped tarragon and serve in warmed bowls, with crusty bread if you like.

**as a main course**    Increase all the ingredient quantities by half. Serve each portion of ragout topped with a seared thick slice of fois gras, or a pan-fried small cod fillet, or 1 or 2 fried good quality butcher's sausages.

# Gazpacho consommé with scallop ravioli

SERVES 4

*1kg vine-ripened tomatoes,
    roughly chopped*

*1 small red onion, peeled and
    roughly diced*

*½ red chilli, deseeded and
    chopped*

*1 small garlic clove, peeled and
    crushed*

*1 red pepper, cored, deseeded and
    roughly chopped*

*1 cucumber*

*50ml red wine vinegar*

*135ml tomato juice*

*10g salt*

*100ml olive oil*

*30g coriander leaves*

*20g sugar*

**scallop ravioli (optional)**

*300g fresh pasta (page 157), or
    300g pack wonton wrappers*

*12 queen scallops, corals removed*

*1 egg, beaten*

**to serve**

*1 tomato, skinned, deseeded and
    finely diced*

*4 tbsp olive oil*

*about 20 small basil leaves*

**gazpacho base**  Put the tomatoes into a large bowl with the onion, chilli, garlic and red pepper. Peel the cucumber, halve lengthways and scoop out the seeds. Roughly chop the cucumber flesh and add to the tomatoes. Add the wine vinegar, tomato juice, salt, olive oil, coriander and sugar. Using a hand-held stick blender, slowly break up the ingredients. Increase the speed and whiz for about 3 minutes to make a smooth, thick soup. Cover and leave in the fridge overnight to let the flavours develop.

**to clarify**  The next morning, pour the soup into a muslin-lined strainer set over a large clean bowl. Put this into the fridge and leave undisturbed to allow the liquid to slowly drip through the muslin. This will take about 3 hours; don't be tempted to squeeze the muslin to hasten the process or the liquid will be cloudy. Once it has dripped through, you should have about 800ml clear, intensely flavoured consommé. Discard the residue.

**scallop ravioli**  Bring a large pan of salted water to the boil and have a bowl of iced water ready. Meanwhile, roll out the pasta if using, to a 2mm thickness. Cut out 24 small discs, 4cm in diameter, from the pasta or wonton wrappers. Place a scallop in the centre of half of the discs and brush the pasta or wonton edges lightly with beaten egg. Top with the remaining discs and gently press down around the edges to seal the ravioli, pressing out the air bubbles. Blanch the ravioli in the boiling water for 45 seconds, then remove and refresh in the iced water. Drain on kitchen paper, then cover and refrigerate until needed.

**to serve**  Pour the consommé into a saucepan and heat gently until just hot, but not simmering. Slip in the scallop ravioli and gently warm through in the soup for about 1 minute. Ladle the soup into warmed bowls, placing 3 ravioli in each bowl. Add the diced tomato and drizzle 1 tbsp olive oil over each serving. Scatter the basil leaves on top and serve immediately.

**to serve as a classic gazpacho**  Before clarifying, this is a flavourful classic gazpacho with a good, thick texture that can easily be upsized to serve larger gatherings. Omit the ravioli and stir the soup well after macerating in the fridge overnight. To serve, pour the chilled soup into bowls and add a drizzle of basil oil (page 47). Accompany with small bowls of croûtons, diced sweet onions and red peppers, for guests to help themselves.

# Caramelised onion and mushroom tarts

SERVES 4

### shallot stock
*20g unsalted butter*
*3 shallots, peeled and finely*
   *chopped*
*2 garlic cloves, peeled*
*5 thyme sprigs*
*500ml vegetable nage or chicken*
   *stock (page 156)*

### caramelised onions
*50g unsalted butter*
*1 garlic clove, peeled*
*2 onions, peeled and thinly sliced*
*salt and pepper*

### tart bases
*250g ready-made puff pastry*
   *(thawed if frozen)*
*2 tsp thyme leaves (optional)*
*1 egg, beaten with 1 tsp water*

### mushroom topping
*400g mixed mushrooms, such as*
   *button, chanterelles, shiitake and*
   *oyster, cleaned*
*65g unsalted butter, chilled*
*2 garlic cloves, peeled*
*1 tbsp double cream*
*1–2 tarragon sprigs, chopped, plus*
   *extra to garnish*
*squeeze of lemon juice, to taste*

**shallot stock**    Heat the butter in a pan over a low heat. Add the shallots, garlic and thyme, then cover and sweat gently for 5–7 minutes until soft but not coloured. Add the stock and simmer for 15 minutes. Take off the heat and leave to infuse for 15 minutes. Discard the garlic and thyme; measure 200ml stock. (Any remaining shallot stock can be frozen.)

**caramelised onions**    Melt the butter with the garlic clove in a heavy-based frying pan, then add the onions with a pinch of salt. Cook over a very low heat until the onions are softened and caramelised; this will take between 45 minutes and 1 hour. When finished they should be deep golden in colour, with a sweet, rich taste. Season and discard the garlic. Allow to cool.

**for the tart bases**    Preheat the oven to 220°C (210°C fan oven) Gas 7. Roll out the pastry to a 3mm thickness and cut out four 12cm discs, using a small side plate as a guide. Prick the discs evenly with a fork and place on a baking tray lined with baking parchment. Spoon the caramelised onions on top of the pastry and spread out to a thin even layer, leaving a 5mm clear border. Sprinkle with the thyme if using. Lightly brush the pastry border with the egg wash. Bake for 12–16 minutes until the pastry edges are risen and evenly golden. Carefully transfer the tarts to a wire rack.

**mushroom topping**    While the tart bases are in the oven, halve or slice any larger mushrooms. Heat 50g butter in a frying pan over a medium heat until just foaming. Add the garlic and mushrooms and cook for 2–3 minutes until lightly golden. Season with salt and pepper. Add the 200ml shallot stock and bubble to reduce by two-thirds. Add the cream and then stir in the remaining cold butter, a piece at a time. Stir in the chopped tarragon and a squeeze of lemon juice; check the seasoning and discard the garlic.

**to assemble**    Place the warm tart bases on warmed plates. Spoon the mushrooms on top, piling them up in the middle. Spoon the sauce over and garnish with tarragon to serve.

**as a main course** Bake 2 rather than
4 pastry discs, making them larger. Pan-fry a 1.5kg
chicken 'crown' (ie legs removed) in a little oil until
well browned, then roast at 230°C (220°C fan oven)
Gas 8 for 20 minutes or until cooked through. Rest
for 10 minutes, then carve each breast horizontally
into thick slices. Halve the pastry discs and place
on warmed plates. Spoon on the mushrooms,
mushroom sauce and chicken. Garnish with
tarragon and serve with garlic purée (page 136).

# Swede & potato gratin with pine nuts

SERVES 4

*100g pine nuts*
*200ml milk*
*300ml double cream*
*1 rosemary sprig*
*1 thyme sprig, plus extra to garnish*
*4 garlic cloves, peeled*
*knob of butter*
*2 swede, each about 300g*
*1 or 2 large white potatoes, about
   450g in total*
*salt*

**toasting the pine nuts**    Preheat the oven to 190°C (180°C fan oven) Gas 5. Scatter the pine nuts on a baking tray and toast in the oven for 4–5 minutes until lightly golden.

**infusing the creamy milk**    Pour the milk and cream into a large saucepan and add the rosemary, thyme, garlic and a third of the pine nuts. Place over a low heat to infuse for 20 minutes. Take off the heat, then cover and leave to infuse for a further 30 minutes. Strain the creamy milk, discarding the pine nuts, garlic and herbs.

**preparing the gratin**    Grease a medium-small ovenproof dish, about 4–5cm deep, with the butter. Peel the swede and potatoes, then cut lengthways into 3mm slices, using a mandoline or a sharp knife. Arrange a layer of swede slices in the bottom of the prepared dish, drizzle with a little of the creamy milk and add a pinch of salt. Cover with a layer of potato slices, then a little more creamy milk and a sprinkling of salt. Continue alternating the layers in this way until the dish is almost full, then finish with a layer of creamy milk.

**to bake**    Cover the dish with foil and bake for 50 minutes – 1 hour until the gratin is cooked through. Test by inserting a metal skewer or a small knife in the centre; it should meet with little resistance. Remove the foil and bake for a further 10 minutes until the top layer is tinged golden brown. Leave to stand for 10–15 minutes before serving.

**to serve**    Spoon a neat portion of gratin on to each warmed plate and sprinkle with the remaining toasted pine nuts. Garnish with thyme sprigs and serve.

**note**    This gratin is an excellent accompaniment to chicken, duck and game, including venison.

# Terrine of herb-cooked leeks & crab salad

SERVES 8

**terrine**

*2 litres vegetable nage (page 156),
    prepared a day in advance*

*small bunch of tarragon*

*5 thyme sprigs*

*3 tbsp unsalted butter*

*salt and pepper*

*12 large leeks, white part only*

**crab salad**

*100g white crab meat*

*3 tbsp mayonnaise*

*1 tbsp chopped chives*

*squeeze of lemon juice, to taste*

**to finish**

*4 vine-ripened tomatoes, sliced*

**cooking the leeks**   Bring the vegetable nage to a simmer in a large pan with the tarragon, thyme, butter and seasoning. Allow to infuse over a very low heat for 15 minutes. Add the leeks to the nage and cover with a disc of greaseproof paper (that fits snugly in the pan). Simmer gently for 15–20 minutes until the leeks are tender. Remove from the heat and leave the leeks to cool in the liquor. When cool, remove with a slotted spoon and drain on kitchen paper.

**preparing the terrine**   Line the inside of a 20 x 7.5cm terrine mould or loaf tin with cling film, leaving an overhang of 10–12cm all round. Put a layer of leeks in the base of the mould and press down firmly. Continue to layer the leeks in the mould until all of them have been used. Fold the overhanging cling film over and place a small tray or rectangular plate on top (that just fits inside the tin). Place a couple of packets of butter (or something similar) on top to press the terrine lightly. Refrigerate overnight.

**crab salad**   Flake the crab meat into a bowl and fold in the mayonnaise, chopped chives and lemon juice to taste.

**to serve**   Carefully remove the terrine from the mould and cut into 1.5cm thick slices, using a very sharp knife. Peel away the cling film from the edges of each slice, then arrange the terrine slices on serving plates or a large platter. Top with the crab salad and tomato slices to serve.

**as a main course**   Serve the terrine with tea-smoked salmon or poached salmon and the crab salad. Tea-smoke 6 salmon fillets, about 140g each, (following the instructions on page 92), or poach the salmon fillets gently in fish stock with a slice of lemon added until just cooked. Allow to cool, then serve with the sliced leek terrine and crab salad.

# Anchovy & tomato terrine with basil purée

SERVES 8–10

*20 large vine-ripened tomatoes*
*olive oil, to drizzle*
*salt*
*1 tsp icing sugar*
*3 garlic cloves, peeled and thinly*
*    sliced*
*small bunch of thyme*
*3 1/2 sheets of leaf gelatine*
*250ml vegetable nage (page 156),*
*    see note*
*250g white anchovies in oil,*
*    drained*
*bunch of basil (about 40 leaves),*
*    stems removed*

**to serve**
*basil oil (see page 47)*

**confit tomato**    Preheat the oven to 120°C (110°C fan oven) Gas 1/4. Make a small cross incision on the base of each tomato, immerse in boiling water for 5 seconds, then remove and refresh in iced water. Peel away the skins, quarter the tomatoes and scoop out the seeds. Arrange the tomato 'petals' on a baking tray lined with baking parchment. Drizzle with a little olive oil, dust lightly with salt and icing sugar, then scatter over the sliced garlic and thyme sprigs. Put into the oven for 3–4 hours until the tomatoes are deep red in colour and very wrinkled. When ready, pick out the tomato 'petals' and set aside.

**making the jellied nage**    Pre-soak the gelatine leaves in cold water to cover for 15 minutes. Warm 50ml of the vegetable nage in a small saucepan until hot, then take off the heat. Squeeze out excess water from the soaked gelatine sheets, add them to the hot liquid and stir to dissolve. Now add the remaining cool nage and allow to cool.

**assembling the terrine**    Line a terrine mould or small loaf tin, measuring about 20 x 7.5cm with two layers of cling film, leaving plenty overhanging. Pour in a little of the jellied nage to cover the bottom thinly. Arrange a layer of tomato 'petals' in the mould, followed by a layer of anchovies, then a sprinkling of basil leaves and spoon over a little of the jellied nage on top. Repeat these layers to use up all of these ingredients. Fold the overlapping cling film over, press firmly and place a small tray or rectangular plate on top (that just fits inside the tin). Place a couple of packets of butter (or something similar) on top to press the terrine lightly. Refrigerate overnight.

**to serve**    Tip the terrine out of the mould on to a serving plate and remove the cling film. Streak the plate with the basil oil. To serve, cut the terrine into slices with a warm knife and accompany with the basil oil.

**note**    If you happen to have any gazpacho consommé (page 105) to hand, use this in place of the herb nage – the flavour is sublime.

# Blinis topped with curried oysters

*Illustrated on page 112*

*Illustrated on page 112*

**SERVES 6–8**

**blinis**
450g waxy potatoes, such as
    La Ratte
salt
1 tbsp plain flour
1½ tbsp crème fraîche (at room
    temperature)
1 tbsp chopped chives
1 tbsp chopped dill
1 egg, plus 2 egg yolks

**curry sauce**
50g butter
2 shallots, peeled and finely sliced
80g fennel, trimmed and finely
    sliced
50ml white wine
200ml fish or vegetable stock
2 tbsp crème fraîche
1 tsp medium curry powder
squeeze of lemon juice, to taste

**to assemble**
20–24 large rock oysters, cleaned
    (see page 48) and shelled
1 tbsp vegetable oil
25g butter
20g coriander leaves

**blini batter**    Put the potatoes into a medium pan, cover with cold water and add salt. Bring to a simmer and simmer for about 20 minutes until tender. Drain the potatoes, then peel while still hot, using a small knife. Press them through a fine sieve or potato ricer. Weigh 300g and put into a large bowl. Add the flour to the warm potato and whisk until smooth, then whisk in the crème fraîche and chopped herbs. Finally add the whole egg and extra yolks and continue to whisk until the mixture is very smooth. Cover the bowl and leave the blini batter to rest for at least 15 minutes.

**curry sauce**    Melt 25g of the butter in a small pan. Add the shallots and fennel with a pinch of salt, stir, then cover and sweat gently for about 10 minutes until soft but not coloured. Add the white wine to the pan and bubble to reduce by two-thirds. Add the stock, crème fraîche and curry powder and simmer over a low heat for 5 minutes. Remove from the heat, pass through a fine sieve and set aside until ready to use.

**to cook the blinis**    Heat a large non-stick frying pan over a medium heat. Add the oil, then the butter, and heat until melted and light brown in colour. Cook the blinis in batches, 5 or 6 at a time. Drop tablespoonfuls of the blini batter into the pan, spacing them well apart, and cook for 1 minute on each side until golden brown. Drain on kitchen paper and keep warm while cooking the rest. You should have enough batter for 20–24 blinis.

**to finish**    Bring the curry sauce back to the boil, add the oysters and simmer for 1 minute. Arrange 3 blinis on each warmed plate. Using a slotted spoon, lift the oysters out of the sauce and set aside. Put the curry sauce back on a high heat and whisk in the remaining 25g butter in pieces. Add a squeeze of lemon juice and check the seasoning. Place an oyster on each blini, spoon the curry sauce over and around, and top with the coriander leaves. Serve immediately.

## as a canapé    *Illustrated on page 113*

*Illustrated on page 113*

Make smaller blinis, allowing 2 tsp batter each, and cook as above. Cut in half and sandwich together with different fillings. Try the following: Parma ham and soft cream cheese; blue Stilton garnished with chervil or parsley; smoked salmon with crème fraîche and a little salmon caviar.

# Creamed salt cod & celeriac soup

SERVES 6

*50g salt cod*
*75g unsalted butter*
*1 onion, peeled and finely diced*
*1 garlic clove, peeled and crushed*
*150g celeriac, peeled and roughly diced*
*750ml chicken stock (page 156)*
*250ml double cream*
*salt and pepper*
*1 tbsp chopped chives*

**preparing the salt cod**   Soak the salt cod 24 hours in advance – in plenty of cold water to remove excess salt.

**softening the vegetables**   Melt the butter in a medium saucepan over a low heat. Add the onion and garlic, then cover and sweat, stirring occasionally, for about 15 minutes until soft. Add the diced celeriac and continue to sweat for a further 5–7 minutes until the celeriac is softened.

**making the soup**   Drain the salt cod and add to the vegetables with the stock and cream. Bring to a simmer and simmer gently for 15 minutes. Remove from the heat and cool slightly, then whiz in a blender until very smooth. Pass the soup through a fine sieve into a bowl and check the seasoning. Leave to cool, then chill thoroughly.

**to finish**   Serve in chilled bowls, scattered with chopped chives. Accompany with soft bread.

**note**   This soup can be served hot if you prefer. It is also an excellent base for a chowder. Simply poach filleted chunks of fresh fish, such as cod or haddock, in the puréed soup for about 6–8 minutes until cooked, then serve with crusty bread.

# Crab croquettes with tomato dipping sauce

**croquette mix**
*700g potatoes, such as*
*   King Edward*
*salt and pepper*
*25g unsalted butter*
*500g fresh white crab meat*
*2 egg yolks*
*small bunch of dill, leaves stripped*
*   and chopped*

**tomato dipping sauce**
*2 very ripe plum tomatoes, diced*
*1/2 small red onion, finely chopped*
*juice of 1/2 lemon*
*4 tbsp fine quality olive oil*
*2 tbsp chopped basil or marjoram*

**to finish**
*oil, to deep-fry*
*flour, to dust*
*1 egg, beaten with a little water*
*200g dried breadcrumbs*
*sea salt*
*basil leaves, to garnish*

**the croquette mix**    Peel and quarter the potatoes. Put into a pan, add cold salted water to cover and bring to the boil. Cook for 15–20 minutes until tender, then drain thoroughly and leave to stand, uncovered, for 3–4 minutes to dry off excess moisture. While still warm, push the potatoes through a sieve or potato ricer into a large bowl. Mix in the butter, followed by the crab meat, egg yolks and chopped dill. Season with salt and pepper to taste and allow to cool. When cold, roll the mixture into cylinders, about 2cm in diameter and 20cm long. Place on a lightly floured tray and refrigerate for 1 hour.

**tomato dipping sauce**    Combine the diced tomatoes and red onion in a small bowl. Add the lemon juice, olive oil and chopped basil. Toss to mix and season with salt and pepper to taste. Set aside to infuse at room temperature for 30 minutes.

**to fry the croquettes**    Heat the oil for deep frying in a deep-fat fryer or other suitable pan to 180°C. Cut each log into three, to make 6–7cm long croquettes. Roll each one in flour to dust, then dip in egg wash and roll in the breadcrumbs to coat evenly all over. Deep-fry the croquettes, a few at a time, for about 2 minutes until golden brown. Drain on kitchen paper, season with sea salt and keep warm while cooking the rest.

**to serve**    Arrange the croquettes on serving plates and spoon a portion of tomato dipping sauce alongside. Or put them on a large platter with the dipping sauce in a serving bowl. Garnish with basil leaves and serve at once.

**variation**    Alternatively, you can shape the croquette mixture into fish cakes. Dust with flour, dip in egg wash, coat with breadcrumbs and cook as above. Serve in split soft rolls with a few lettuce leaves and tartare sauce, as a tasty snack or light meal.

# Home-cured salmon with grainy mustard dressing

SERVES 8–10

*1 very fresh salmon fillet, skin on, about 1kg*

**cure**

*350g rock salt*

*160g granulated sugar*

*grated zest of 3 lemons*

*grated zest of 3 limes*

*2 star anise, crushed or roughly ground*

*50g chopped mixed herbs, such as dill, tarragon and chives (ie about 1½ cups)*

**mustard dressing**

*2 tbsp wholegrain mustard*

*1 tbsp sugar*

*1½ tbsp white wine vinegar*

*5 tbsp groundnut or vegetable oil*

*1 tsp finely chopped dill*

*salt and pepper*

**to finish**

*lemon wedges*

*dill sprigs*

*rye bread*

**curing the salmon**    This needs to be done a day in advance. Lay the salmon fillet on a board and check for any small pin bones, removing them with tweezers. In a bowl, mix together the rock salt, sugar, citrus zests, crushed star anise and 5 tbsp chopped herbs. Line a tray with cling film, leaving plenty of overhang, and spread the curing mix on top. Place the salmon flesh-side on the curing mix, press to adhere and turn to coat on all sides. Wrap tightly in the cling film, place in the fridge and leave to cure for 24 hours, turning the salmon after 12 hours.

**the next day**    Unwrap the salmon and rinse off the curing mix under cold running water. Pat dry with kitchen paper. Lay skin-side down on a large clean piece of cling film. Scatter the cupful of chopped herbs over the cured salmon flesh to coat evenly and press firmly. Wrap tightly in the cling film, pressing the herbs into the fish, and refrigerate for 2 hours.

**mustard dressing**    Mix the mustard, sugar and wine vinegar together in a bowl. Slowly drizzle in the oil, whisking to emulsify, then stir in the chopped dill and season with salt and pepper to taste. Pour into a small serving dish.

**to serve**    Remove the cling film from the salmon and place on an oblong serving platter with the lemon wedges and mustard dressing alongside. Garnish with dill sprigs. Cut the salmon into thin slices to serve and accompany with rye bread.

**as a canapé**    Serve small slices of home-cured salmon on warm blinis or small rounds of pumpernickel bread, with a touch of crème fraîche and a sprinkling of snipped chives.

# Honey glazed ham with celeriac rémoulade

SERVES 4–6

1 small unsmoked ham knuckle,
    about 1kg
1 onion, peeled and chopped
1 carrot, peeled and chopped
1 celery stick, trimmed and
    chopped
4 garlic cloves, peeled
3 bay leaves
1 thyme sprig
1 parsley sprig
2 cinnamon sticks
10 cloves
5 peppercorns

glaze
20 cloves
60ml port
80g honey
1 tbsp demerara sugar

celeriac rémoulade
1/2 celeriac
4 tbsp mayonnaise (page 157)
squeeze of lemon juice
1/2 tbsp chopped parsley
salt and pepper

**to cook the ham**    Put the ham knuckle into a large pan and cover with cold water. Slowly bring to the boil, then drain off the water. Cover with fresh cold water, bring to the boil and skim. Add the vegetables, garlic, herbs and spices. Simmer gently, skimming frequently, for about 3 hours until the meat is very tender; it should be almost falling from the bone. Take off the heat and leave the ham to cool in the liquor for 30 minutes.

**to glaze the ham**    Preheat the oven to 220°C (210°C fan oven) Gas 7. Remove the ham knuckle from the liquor and place on a board. Carefully remove the outer skin with a sharp knife. Score the fat layer in a trellis pattern, then stud with the cloves and place in a shallow roasting dish. Warm the port and honey together in a small pan, stir until blended, then bring to the boil and pour evenly over the ham. Sprinkle with the demerara sugar and put into the hot oven for 15–20 minutes to glaze, until the surface is rich golden brown in colour. Transfer to a plate and allow to cool.

**celeriac rémoulade**    Peel the celeriac and cut into julienne or matchstick strips. Put into a bowl with the mayonnaise, lemon juice and chopped parsley and toss to mix. Season with salt and pepper to taste and set aside until ready to serve.

**to serve**    Carve the ham into thin slices and arrange on a platter or individual plates. Serve with the celeriac rémoulade and accompany with thin slices of brown bread.

# Oxtail & lentil ragout with root vegetables

SERVES 4

## braised oxtail

*500g oxtail, cut into 5–6cm lengths*
*salt and pepper*
*2–3 tbsp vegetable oil*
*1 carrot, peeled and cut into*
*    quarters*
*1 onion, peeled and cut into*
*    quarters*
*2 garlic cloves, peeled and cracked*
*500ml red wine*
*1 litre chicken stock (page 156)*
*few thyme sprigs*
*1 bay leaf*
*5 black peppercorns*

## lentils

*200g Puy lentils (or other green*
*    lentils)*
*1 carrot, peeled and quartered*
*1 onion, peeled and quartered*
*2 celery sticks, trimmed and*
*    chopped*
*2 garlic cloves, peeled and cracked*
*handful of thyme sprigs*

## to finish

*50g unsalted butter, chilled and*
*    diced*
*50g piece smoked bacon, diced*
*1 shallot, peeled and finely diced*
*3–4 tbsp chopped parsley*

**braised oxtail**    Season the oxtail pieces with salt and pepper. Heat the oil in a large saucepan over a high heat, add the oxtail pieces and sear on all sides until browned all over. Remove with a slotted spoon; set aside. Add the carrot, onion and garlic to the pan and cook gently until softened and golden. Return the oxtail and add the wine. Bubble to reduce by two-thirds, then add the stock, thyme, bay leaf and peppercorns. Bring back to a simmer and simmer gently, skimming occasionally, for $3^{1}/_{2}$ hours until the meat comes away from the bone easily. Leave the oxtail to cool in the liquor. When cool, strain and reserve the liquor, discarding the flavourings. Take the oxtail off the bone and divide the meat into shreds. Keep the meat and liquor to one side until ready to finish the dish.

**to cook the lentils**    Put the lentils into a saucepan, add cold water to cover and bring to the boil, then drain and return to the pan. Repeat this process once more. Add the vegetables, garlic and thyme and cover again with water. Bring to the boil, lower the heat and simmer for 6–8 minutes or until the lentils are al dente, tender but retaining a bite. Remove from the heat and leave to cool in the liquor, then strain off the cooking liquor. Separate the vegetables from the lentils and chop these roughly; discard the garlic.

**to finish**    Heat a third of the butter in a frying pan, add the bacon and fry until golden. Add the shallot and fry gently for 1 minute, then add the shredded oxtail, 300ml of the reserved oxtail liquor, the lentils and chopped vegetables. Bring to the boil and bubble to reduce the liquor by half. Lower the heat and stir in the remaining butter. The consistency should be soupy and rich. Scatter over the chopped parsley and serve in warmed bowls.

**as a main course**    This dish is an excellent winter main course. Simply double up the quantities and leave the oxtail on the bone after braising. Serve with creamy mash.

**as a canapé**    Cut small bread rounds, 2–3cm in diameter, and toast to make croûtons. Top each one with a teaspoonful of oxtail ragout and serve hot.

# Beef bourguignonne tartlets

SERVES 4

**beef bourguignonne**

*450g shin of beef or ox cheek (or braising steak)*

*1 large carrot, peeled and halved lengthways*

*1 large onion, peeled and quartered*

*2 celery sticks, halved*

*4 garlic cloves, peeled and crushed*

*2 bay leaves*

*handful of thyme sprigs*

*400ml red wine*

*3 tbsp unsalted butter*

*60g piece smoked bacon, cut into cubes*

*150g button mushrooms, sliced*

*salt and pepper*

*1 chicken bouillon cube, crumbled*

*2 tbsp vegetable oil*

**caramelised onions**

*60g unsalted butter*

*2 large onions, peeled and thinly sliced*

*2 garlic cloves, peeled and crushed*

**tartlet cases**

*1 quantity shortcrust pastry (page 156)*

*baby spinach or chard leaves, lightly blanched, to garnish*

**marinating the beef**    This needs to be done a day ahead. Cut the meat roughly into 3cm cubes and put into a bowl with the carrot, onion, celery, garlic, bay leaves, thyme sprigs and red wine. Cover and leave to marinate in the fridge overnight.

**the bourguignonne base**    The next day, strain off the wine and reserve. Tip the meat and vegetables on to kitchen paper, separate them (keeping the herbs with the vegetables) and pat dry; set aside. Melt 1 tbsp butter in a large frying pan over a medium heat, add the bacon and fry for 3–4 minutes until golden. Remove with a slotted spoon, drain on kitchen paper and set aside. Melt another 1 tbsp butter in the pan, then add the reserved vegetables with the mushrooms and fry for 7–8 minutes until soft and golden. Drain on kitchen paper and season with a pinch of salt; reserve.

**cooking the beef bourguignonne**    Put the frying pan back on the heat. Season the beef cubes with salt and pepper. Add 1 tbsp butter to the hot pan and, when it is very hot, add the beef cubes. Sear, turning, for 4–5 minutes until browned on all sides. Put the beef into a flameproof casserole or heavy-based pan with the vegetables, bacon, bouillon cube and wine. Bring to a simmer and cook gently, skimming as necessary, for about 3 hours until the meat is very tender and the liquor is reduced right down. Add a little water during cooking if necessary. By the end of the cooking time, the bourguignonne should be nearly dry and the meat should fall into strands easily. If necessary, add a little more water and continue to cook until the meat is ready. Allow to cool, then discard the vegetables and herbs. Break up the meat with a wooden spoon.

**caramelised onions**    Heat a large frying pan over a medium heat and add the butter. When foaming, add the onions and garlic and season with a pinch of salt. Cook slowly for 30–45 minutes until soft and caramelised to a rich golden brown colour. Drain and set aside to cool.

**tarts**    Preheat the oven to 220°C (210°C fan oven) Gas 7. Roll out the shortcrust pastry and cut out four 15cm discs. Use to line individual tartlet cases, trimming away excess pastry. Prick the bases with a fork. Divide the caramelised onions evenly among the pastry cases and bake the tarts for 12–15 minutes until light crisp and golden. Meanwhile, gently reheat the bourguignonne. Spoon the meat into the pastry cases and serve garnished with warm spinach or chard.

**as a main course**  Cook double the quantity of bourguignonne until the meat is tender, but don't break it up after cooking. Cut 4 rectangles of ready-made puff pastry, score with a knife and lay on a baking sheet. Bake at 220°C (210°C fan oven) Gas 7 for 12–15 minutes until crisp and golden. Serve each bourguignonne portion topped with a pastry rectangle and accompanied by broccoli and French beans.

**as a main course** Triple the quantities — you will need a boned and rolled short saddle of lamb, about 1kg. Cook the meat as above, allowing about 30–40 minutes in the oven. Allow to rest for 10 minutes. Carve the meat into thick slices and arrange on warmed plates Serve with the minted peas and roasted new potatoes, omitting the Parmesan. Garnish with mint leaves.

# Roasted lamb cannelloni with minted peas

**SERVES 6**

*1 pair of lamb chumps, off the
    bone, 400–500g*

*salt and pepper*

*1 tbsp olive oil*

*2 tbsp unsalted butter*

*1 carrot, peeled and roughly
    chopped*

*1 onion, peeled and roughly
    chopped*

*1 thyme sprig*

*1 rosemary sprig*

*2 shallots, peeled and finely
    chopped*

*100g podded peas*

*10g (½ cup) mint leaves, roughly
    chopped*

**to finish**

*50g Parmesan cheese, finely pared
    into shavings*

**to cook the lamb**    Preheat the oven to 220°C (210°C fan oven) Gas 7. Season the lamb all over with salt and pepper. Heat a medium frying pan with a metal handle (suitable for use in the oven) over a high heat. Add the olive oil followed by 1 tbsp of butter and heat until golden brown. Add the lamb and let it colour for 1 minute, then turn and repeat to colour lightly on all sides. Remove the meat from the pan and set aside. Add the carrot, onion, thyme and rosemary to the pan, then place the meat on top of the vegetables. Roast in the oven for 8–10 minutes for medium-rare meat, then leave to rest in a warm place for 10 minutes.

**minted peas**    Add the peas to a pan of boiling water and simmer for 3 minutes or until tender. Drain and toss with the remaining butter, shallots and chopped mint. Season with salt and pepper to taste.

**to serve**    Using a very sharp knife, cut the lamb into very thin slices. Lay one slice flat on a board and season lightly with salt and pepper, then add a spoonful of peas, scattering them along the width. Roll the meat around the peas and secure with a cocktail stick. Repeat to use all the lamb slices. Arrange on individual plates, or a platter, and scatter over any remaining peas. Sprinkle with Parmesan shavings and serve.

# posh

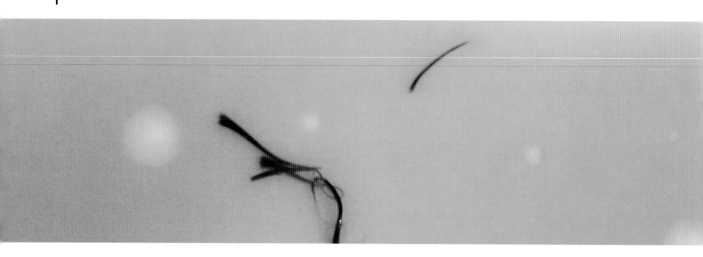

Asparagus tagliatelle with morel cream & chervil

Truffle & white bean soup

Lime marinated scallop ceviche

Roasted scallops with asparagus & parsnip sauce

Creamed leeks with langoustines

Langoustines with garlic purée

Crab with avocado & sesame filo wafers

Crab & salmon tortellini in ginger crab bisque

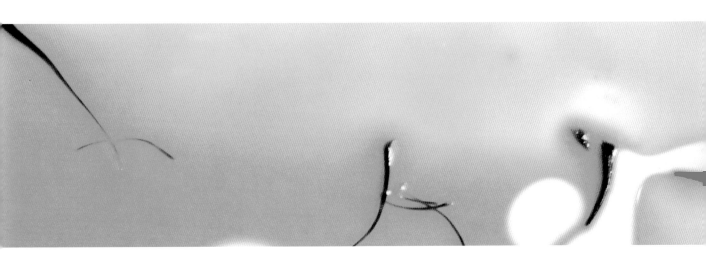

Red mullet on fennel with vanilla & olive sauce

Roasted quail, cabbage and chanterelle soup

Chicken with cep & artichoke carpaccio

Breast of wood pigeon with beetroot vinaigrette

Terrine of foie gras, wood pigeon & ham hock

Foie gras poached in Sauternes with peas

Open ravioli of rabbit with mustard sauce

Seared veal carpaccio

# Asparagus tagliatelle with morel cream & chervil

SERVES 4

**asparagus tagliatelle**
*12–16 thick asparagus spears*

**morel cream**
*40g dried morels, or other dried
    wild mushrooms*
*20g unsalted butter*
*3 shallots, peeled and finely diced*
*3 garlic cloves, peeled and cracked*
*salt and pepper*
*150ml rich Madeira*
*50ml double cream*
*squeeze of lemon juice, to taste*
*1 tbsp tarragon leaves, chopped*
*16 small chervil sprigs*

**to soak the dried morels**    Bring 800ml water to the boil in a pan, then add the dried mushrooms and take the pan off the heat. Cover and set aside to soak for about 45 minutes until the mushrooms are soft. Drain, reserving the liquid.

**tagliatelle**    Trim the woody stalk ends from the asparagus spears and peel the lower ends of the stalks. Slice the asparagus lengthways, using a mandoline or swivel vegetable peeler, into very thin strips to make 'tagliatelle'. Cover with cling film and refrigerate until needed.

**morel cream**    Melt the butter in a medium pan over a low heat, then add the shallots and garlic with a pinch of salt. Stir, then cover and sweat gently, stirring occasionally, for 10 minutes or until the shallots are soft and translucent but not coloured. Add the Madeira, increase the heat to medium-high and bubble to reduce by two-thirds. Add the softened mushrooms, 75ml of the reserved mushroom water, the cream and another pinch of salt. Bring to a simmer and let the sauce bubble gently for 5–7 minutes to reduce and thicken slightly. Check that the mushrooms have softened sufficiently. If not, add another tbsp mushroom water and simmer for a further minute or two. When ready, remove from the heat, and check the seasoning. Add a squeeze of lemon juice and stir in the chopped tarragon. Keep warm until ready to serve.

**to serve**    Add the asparagus tagliatelle to a pan of boiling salted water and blanch for 2 minutes. Drain thoroughly and arrange on warmed plates. Spoon the morel cream over and around the asparagus. Scatter with the sprigs of chervil and serve.

**note**    When in season, buy fresh morels instead; you will need 100g. Clean thoroughly, but do not soak. Sauté lightly in a little butter before adding to the shallots.

# Truffle & white bean soup

SERVES 6

*100g haricot or cannellini beans,
    soaked in cold water overnight*
*1 whole garlic bulb*
*1 onion, peeled and quartered*
*1 carrot, peeled and quartered*
*1 sprig each of rosemary, thyme
    and parsley*
*200g piece smoked bacon*
*2 litres chicken stock (page 156)*
*100g unsalted butter*
*4 shallots, peeled and finely
    chopped*
*1 lemon thyme sprig*
*150ml double cream*
*1 tbsp truffle oil, plus extra
    to drizzle*

**to cook the beans**    Drain the pre-soaked beans, put them into a large saucepan and cover with fresh cold water. Bring to the boil, then drain and return the beans to the pan. Cut the garlic bulb in half crossways (through the cloves) and add one half to the pan with the onion, carrot, rosemary, thyme and parsley. Roughly chop half of the bacon and add to the pan. Pour in the stock, bring to a simmer and cook until the beans are tender, about 1½–2 hours. Drain the beans, reserving the cooking liquor. Discard the herb sprigs, vegetables and garlic.

**the soup base**    Peel and finely chop the other half of the garlic. Dice the remaining bacon. Melt 80g of the butter in a large pan, then add the chopped garlic, diced bacon, shallots and lemon thyme. Stir, then cover and sweat over a low heat for about 15 minutes until the shallots are soft but not coloured.

**the puréed soup**    Now add the reserved bean cooking liquor to the soup base, together with half of the beans and the cream. Simmer gently for 15 minutes, then remove from the heat. Cool slightly, then tip into a blender and whiz until smooth. Pass through a fine sieve into a clean pan or bowl. Adjust the seasoning, then stir in the truffle oil. (The soup can be prepared ahead to this stage and kept in the fridge for up to 2 days; refrigerate the whole beans separately.)

**to serve**    Melt the remaining 20g butter in a medium pan, add the remaining whole beans and warm through. Heat the soup in a separate pan. Spoon the hot buttery beans into the centre of 6 warmed serving bowls and pour the hot puréed soup over them to cover. Finish with droplets of truffle oil. Serve at once.

**as a canapé**   Serve small portions in coffee cups. Halve the quantities for 8–10 canapé-sized portions. Whiz the soup, using a hand-held stick blender to froth just before pouring into the cups and top with a sprinkling of chopped chives.

# Lime marinated scallop ceviche

SERVES 4

*8 large scallops*
*sea salt*

marinade
*2 vine-ripened tomatoes*
*¼ cucumber*
*1 tbsp finely diced shallot*
*finely grated zest of 1 lime*
*juice of 1–2 limes*
*4 tbsp fish or vegetable stock*
*1 tsp sugar*
*10 basil leaves, chopped*
*10 coriander leaves, roughly torn*
*150ml extra virgin olive oil*

**preparing the scallops**  Chill 4 deep serving plates in the fridge for 20 minutes. Meanwhile, open the scallops. Insert the point of a strong knife between the shells near the hinge and twist to prise the shells apart. Take out the scallop and discard the grey membrane. Remove the coral from the nugget of white scallop meat. Slice each scallop horizontally into 4 thin rounds and arrange 8 slices on each of the chilled plates. Lightly season the scallops with a little sea salt.

**preparing the marinade**  Make a small cross incision on the base of each tomato, immerse in boiling water for 5 seconds, then remove and refresh in iced water. Peel away the skins, quarter the tomatoes and scoop out the seeds, then cut the flesh into small dice and place in a bowl. Peel the cucumber, halve lengthways and scoop out the seeds, then cut the flesh into small dice and add to the tomatoes. Add the shallot, lime zest, the juice of 1 lime, the stock, sugar, herbs and olive oil. Adjust the sweet and sour balance, adding a little extra lime juice or sugar to taste.

**to marinate**  Spoon the marinade evenly over the scallops, cover the bowls with cling film and leave to marinate at cool room temperature for 15 minutes.

**to serve**  Uncover the scallop ceviche, check the seasoning and serve.

# Roasted scallops with asparagus & parsnip sauce

SERVES 4

*8–12 large fresh scallops, shelled,
    corals removed (see page 133)*

*12 asparagus spears*

*salt and pepper*

*3 tbsp olive oil*

*1 tbsp unsalted butter*

*squeeze of lemon juice*

**parsnip sauce**

*1 tsp cumin seeds*

*175g parsnips*

*1 tbsp unsalted butter*

*300ml chicken stock (page 156)*

*50ml double cream*

**parsnip sauce**    Make this first. Heat a small frying pan until hot, then add the cumin seeds and toast for 45 seconds – 1 minute until lightly coloured. Tip on to a board and crush with the back of a heavy knife. Peel the parsnips, quarter lengthways and remove the woody cores, then roughly chop the flesh. Melt the butter in a pan and add the parsnips and cumin. Stir, then cover and sweat for about 25 minutes until very soft. Add two-thirds of the stock, then stir in the cream and bring to a simmer. Cook gently for 5 minutes, then transfer to a blender and whiz until very smooth, adding a little more stock if necessary to achieve a pouring consistency. Pass through a fine sieve into a clean pan and set aside.

**blanching the asparagus**    Trim the woody ends from the asparagus and peel the lower end of the stalks. Add the asparagus to a pan of boiling salted water and blanch for 2–3 minutes. Drain and refresh in cold water.

**pan-frying the scallops**    Carefully cut each scallop in half horizontally into 2 discs and season with salt and pepper. Heat a large frying pan over a medium-high heat. When hot, add the olive oil, then the butter. When it is sizzling, add the scallop discs in a single layer and cook for 30 seconds. Turn and cook the other side for 30 seconds. Immediately remove and drain on kitchen paper, then sprinkle with a little lemon juice.

**to assemble**    While pan-frying the scallops, reheat the parsnip sauce and, if necessary, warm the asparagus briefly in the microwave. Arrange the scallops in the centre of warmed plates, top with the asparagus and spoon over the parsnip sauce. Serve immediately.

# Creamed leeks with langoustines

SERVES 4

16 langoustines or large prawns,
   shelled and cleaned
2 large leeks (white part only)
salt and pepper
100ml double cream
3 garlic cloves, peeled and cracked
4 tsp finely chopped chives
lemon juice, to taste
2 tbsp olive oil
25g unsalted butter

**preparing the langoustines**   Rinse the langoustines, pat dry with kitchen paper and set aside.

**creamed leeks**   Quarter the leeks lengthways and slice finely. Add to a pan of boiling salted water and blanch for 3–4 minutes until tender. Drain and refresh in iced water, then drain thoroughly. Put the cream, garlic and leeks into a clean pan and bring to a simmer. Let bubble until reduced by about two-thirds to a rich, thick sauce; discard the garlic. Season with salt and pepper to taste, stir in the chives and finish with a squeeze of lemon juice. Set the creamed leeks aside; keep warm.

**pan-frying the langoustines**   Heat a large non-stick frying pan over a high heat. Season the langoustines with a little salt. When the pan is hot, add the olive oil, then the butter. When it is sizzling, add the langoustines and sauté quickly for a minute or two until golden brown. Remove and drain on kitchen paper. Finish with a squeeze of lemon juice.

**to serve**   Spoon the leek sauce into the centre of warmed serving plates. Top with the langoustines and serve, with slices of crusty baguette.

## as individual tarts   Buy 16 small cooked prawns rather than langoustines. Prepare the creamed leeks as above. Line four 10cm individual tart tins with shortcrust pastry (page 156). Prick the bases with a fork, line with greaseproof paper and baking beans, cover and rest in the fridge for 30 minutes. Bake the tart cases blind at 200°C (190°C fan oven) Gas 6 for 15–20 minutes until golden brown and crisp. Leave to firm up for a few minutes, then fill with the creamed leeks and top with the prawns. Warm in the oven for 5–10 minutes before serving if necessary.

# Langoustines with garlic purée

SERVES 4

*16 langoustines or large prawns,*
*   shelled and cleaned*
*salt and pepper*
*1 tbsp olive oil*
*50g butter*
*1 tsp chopped thyme*
*2 tsp flaked almonds*
*lemon juice, to taste*
*garlic purée*
*3 garlic bulbs*
*200ml double cream*

**preparing the langoustines**   Rinse the langoustines, pat dry with kitchen paper and set aside.

**garlic purée**   Separate the garlic cloves, peel and put into a small saucepan. Cover with cold water and bring to the boil, then drain; repeat this process three times, then return the garlic to the pan. Pour in the cream, add a pinch of salt, and bring to a slow simmer. Let bubble gently stirring occasionally, until the cream is reduced and the garlic is soft. Tip into a blender and whiz until smooth. Pass through a sieve into a bowl, check the seasoning and keep warm.

**to cook the langoustines**   Heat a large non-stick frying pan over a high heat. Season the langoustines with a little salt. When the pan is hot, add the olive oil, then the butter. When it is sizzling, add the langoustines and sauté quickly for 30 seconds, then add the thyme and almonds and sauté for a further minute until golden brown. Remove and drain on kitchen paper. Finish with a squeeze of lemon juice.

**to serve**   Arrange the langoustines with the thyme and almonds on warmed plates. Spoon the garlic purée into small serving bowls and place alongside for dipping. Serve immediately.

**prawn skewers**   Buy 20–24 raw tiger prawns (cleaned and heads removed) rather than langoustines. Thread the prawns on to pre-soaked wooden kebab skewers and pan-fry in olive oil with the thyme and almonds for about 1 minute on each side until the prawns are pink. Serve the prawn skewers with the pan juices spooned over, garnished with wild garlic leaves or thyme sprigs. Accompany with the garlic purée.

# Crab with avocado & sesame filo wafers

SERVES 4

*400g white crab meat*

*10ml olive oil*

*5 basil leaves, finely chopped*

*20 coriander leaves, finely chopped*

*salt*

tomato dressing

*1 very ripe tomato*

*squeeze of lemon juice*

*2 tbsp olive oil*

*pinch of sugar*

*salt and pepper*

sesame filo wafers

*1–2 sheets of filo pastry (thawed if frozen)*

*2 tbsp melted butter*

*10g sesame seeds, toasted*

avocado crème fraîche

*2 ripe avocados*

*50g crème fraîche*

*squeeze of lemon juice*

to finish

*frisée (pale leaves only)*

*small coriander sprigs*

**crab meat**     Flake the crab meat into a bowl, checking that there are no small fragments of shell. Add the olive oil and chopped herbs, toss to mix and season with a little salt to taste.

**tomato dressing**     Cut the tomato in half and press through a fine sieve into a bowl; you should have about 50ml clear rosy tomato water. Add the lemon juice, olive oil and sugar. Season with salt and pepper to taste. Cover and refrigerate.

**sesame filo wafers**     Preheat the oven to 190°C (180°C fan oven) Gas 5. Using a 6cm metal cutter, cut 12 rounds from the filo pastry. Lay the filo rounds on a baking sheet lined with non-stick baking parchment. Lightly brush with butter and sprinkle with the toasted sesame seeds. Cover with another sheet of parchment and then invert another baking sheet on top to weigh it down. Bake for about 8–10 minutes until golden and crisp. Carefully remove from the hot baking sheets and allow the filo wafers to cool on the paper.

**avocado crème fraîche**     Peel, halve and stone the avocado, then roughly chop the flesh. Put into a blender with 4 tsp cold water and whiz until smooth. Transfer to a bowl and fold in the crème fraîche. Add the lemon juice and season with salt to taste. Cover the surface closely with cling film to prevent discolouration.

**to assemble**     Arrange little towers on serving plates, alternating the crab meat and avocado crème fraîche between sesame filo wafers. Top with a little pile of frisée and a few coriander sprigs. Surround with the tomato dressing and serve.

# Crab & salmon tortellini in ginger crab bisque

SERVES 8

### bisque
400g crab shells and/or prawn
    shells, broken
2 tbsp olive oil
1/2 onion, peeled and roughly
    chopped
3 garlic cloves, peeled and cracked
50g piece root ginger, peeled and
    grated
1 carrot, peeled and roughly
    chopped
1/4 fennel bulb, roughly chopped
1 celery stick, trimmed and
    roughly chopped
3–4 thyme sprigs
1 tsp fennel seeds
1 tsp coriander seeds
1 tbsp tomato purée
200ml double cream
salt and pepper
lemon juice, to taste

### tortellini
300g fresh pasta (page 157), or
    300g pack wonton wrappers
600g fresh salmon fillet, skinned
100ml single cream
400g picked white crab meat
20 basil leaves, chopped
1 egg yolk
juice of 1/2 lemon
1 egg, beaten with a little milk
    (egg wash)

**preparing the bisque**    Preheat the oven to 190°C (180°C fan oven) Gas 5. Put the shells into a roasting tin and roast for 6–8 minutes, then set aside to cool. Heat the olive oil in a large saucepan and add the onion, garlic, ginger, carrot, fennel, celery, thyme and seeds. Stir, then cover and sweat gently for 15 minutes until the vegetables soften. Stir in the tomato purée and cook for 1 minute, then add the roasted shells and 2 litres water. Bring to a simmer and gently simmer for 30 minutes, skimming occasionally. Strain the liquor into a clean pan and bring to the boil. Let bubble to reduce by two-thirds, to about 500ml. Stir in the cream and bring back to a simmer. Strain again, through a fine sieve. Season with salt and pepper and add a squeeze of lemon juice to taste. Set aside until ready to serve.

**tortellini filling**    Chill your food processor bowl in the fridge. In the meantime, check the salmon for any small bones and remove with tweezers, then cut into 5mm dice. Put 120g of the salmon into the chilled food processor bowl with the cream and a pinch of salt and blend for about 1 minute to a fine paste. Transfer to a mixing bowl and add the crab, remaining salmon, basil, egg yolk and lemon juice. Mix well to combine and season with salt and pepper.

**shaping the tortellini**    If using pasta, cut into 10cm squares; you will need 32 in total. Lay the pasta squares or wonton wrappers flat on a surface and put 1 tbsp of filling in the centre of each square. Lightly brush the edges of the pasta or wontons with egg wash, then fold opposite corner to corner – to form triangles. Press out any trapped air and pinch the edges tightly to seal. Bring two corners together to form a cone and press the tips together.

**cooking the tortellini**    Add the tortellini to a large pan of boiling water, bring back to the boil and cook for 1 1/2 minutes to ensure the pasta and filling have cooked through.

**to serve**    While the tortellini are cooking, bring the bisque back to a simmer over a medium heat, then whiz with a hand-held stick blender to froth up. Ladle into warmed bowls. Drain the tortellini and divide among the bowls. Serve at once.

**note**    The bisque can be served on its own without the tortellini.

# Red mullet on fennel with vanilla & olive sauce

*Illustrated on page 142*

SERVES 4

2 small fennel bulbs, about 200g
  in total
lemon juice, to taste
4 tbsp olive oil
salt and pepper
100g unsalted butter, chilled
20 green olives
½ vanilla pod, split lengthways
700ml fish stock or vegetable nage
  (page 156)
75ml double cream
4 red mullet fillets, about 125g each

**fennel salad**    Trim the fennel, reserving a few feathery fronds for garnish if you like, and slice the bulbs thinly. Put a quarter of the sliced fennel in a bowl with a squeeze of lemon juice and 2 tbsp of the olive oil. Toss to mix and season with salt and pepper. Cover and leave to marinate in the fridge for 40 minutes.

**vanilla and olive sauce**    Melt 75g butter in a small pan over a low heat. When hot, add the remaining fennel, stir, then cover and sweat over a low heat for about 15 minutes until very tender. Meanwhile, remove the stones from half of the olives, slice and set aside, reserving the stones. Scrape out the seeds from the vanilla pod and add to the pan with the empty pod, whole olives and reserved stones. Stir in the stock or nage and bring to the boil. Let bubble for about 20 minutes until reduced by half. Add the cream and simmer for a further 5 minutes. Pass the sauce through a fine sieve into a clean pan and add the sliced olives. Keep warm.

**to cook the red mullet**    Season the fish fillets on both sides with a little salt. Place a large non-stick frying pan over a medium heat. When hot, add the remaining 2 tbsp olive oil. Place the red mullet in the pan, skin-side down, and cook for 1½ minutes. Flip the fillets over and cook for a further 30 seconds. Remove and drain on kitchen paper, then finish with a squeeze of lemon juice.

**to finish the sauce**    While the red mullet is cooking, gently whisk the remaining 25g cold butter into the olive sauce, a piece at a time. Season with a little salt and add a squeeze of lemon juice to taste.

**to serve**    Drain the fennel salad of excess dressing, then arrange in the centre of warmed serving plates. Place the red mullet fillets on top and dress with the vanilla and olive sauce. Serve immediately, garnished with fennel fronds if you like.

## as a main course    *Illustrated on page 143*

Buy 4 sea bass fillets, about 170g each. Pan-fry skin-side down first for 3 minutes, then turn and cook on the other side for 30 seconds – 1 minute until just cooked. Place on warmed plates with hot new potatoes and the fennel salad alongside. Dress with the olive and vanilla sauce and serve.

# Roasted quail, cabbage and chanterelle soup

SERVES 4

### chanterelle soup base

*30g unsalted butter*

*2 shallots, peeled and finely sliced*

*2 thyme sprigs*

*2 tarragon sprigs, plus extra leaves to garnish*

*salt and pepper*

*600ml chicken stock (page 156)*

*125g chanterelles or other wild mushrooms, cleaned*

### roast quail

*4 oven-ready quail, wings removed*

*2 tbsp vegetable oil*

*1 tsp unsalted butter*

### buttered cabbage

*½ small Savoy cabbage, outer leaves removed*

*60g butter*

**making the soup**    Place a small saucepan over a low heat, add half of the butter and heat until melted. Add the shallots with the thyme, tarragon and a pinch of salt. Stir, then cover and sweat gently for 20 minutes until the shallots are soft. Pour in the stock and bring to a simmer. Meanwhile, heat a frying pan over a medium heat, add the rest of the butter and heat until melted. Add the mushrooms and sauté for 2 minutes, then remove and drain on kitchen paper. Add the mushrooms to the soup and simmer for a further 20 minutes, skimming as necessary. Check the seasoning and remove from the heat.

**roasting the quail**    While you are preparing the soup, preheat the oven to 230°C (220°C fan oven) Gas 8 and season the quail with salt and pepper. Heat a frying pan with a metal handle (suitable for use in the oven) over a medium-high heat. Add the oil and when it is smoking hot, add the butter and then the quail. Turn them, using tongs, until lightly caramelised all over, then put the pan into the oven and roast for 5–6 minutes for medium rare, or 8–10 minutes for well done. Transfer to a warm plate and leave to rest for 10 minutes.

**buttered cabbage**    Meanwhile, shred the cabbage into thin ribbons. Add to a pan of boiling salted water and blanch for 4–5 minutes until tender. Immediately refresh in cold water and drain. Place a medium pan over a low heat, add the butter and melt. Add the cabbage, with a pinch of salt and pepper, and sweat gently for about 1 minute. Remove from the heat; keep warm.

**to serve**    Reheat the soup. Remove the quail legs and breasts from the bone (or leave on if serving whole). Place the hot buttered cabbage in the centre of warmed soup plates and top with the quail. Ladle the soup around the cabbage, garnish with tarragon leaves and serve immediately.

# Chicken with cep & artichoke carpaccio

SERVES 2

*2 large globe artichokes*
*1 quantity pickling marinade*
   *(see page 10)*
*2 large ceps (ideally with caps the*
   *same size as the prepared*
   *artichokes), cleaned*
*300ml olive oil*
*6 garlic cloves, peeled and cracked*
*3 thyme sprigs*
*2 bay leaves*
*2 tbsp dried ceps or other dried*
   *wild mushrooms*
*salt and pepper*
*4 inner chicken breast fillets, or*
   *1 small whole skinless breast fillet*
*20g unsalted butter*
*juice of ½ lemon*
*about 20 tarragon leaves*

**pickled artichokes**   Pull off the outer leaves from the artichokes to reveal the hearts, then remove the hairy choke at the base of each one. Bring the pickling marinade to a simmer in a pan, then add the artichoke hearts and simmer for about 5 minutes until just tender. Take off the heat and leave to cool in the marinade, then refrigerate until needed.

**cep confit**   Check that the ceps are thoroughly cleaned and set aside. Put the olive oil, garlic, thyme, bay leaves and dried mushrooms into a pan (that will be just large enough to take the fresh ceps). Add a pinch of salt and allow to infuse for 20 minutes over a very low heat; do not let the garlic colour. Add the whole ceps and ensure that they are completely submerged in the infused oil. Turn the heat up very slightly and allow the mushroom caps to confit in the warm oil over a low heat for 5–6 minutes. Remove the pan from the heat and leave the ceps to cool in the oil.

**sautéed chicken**   Season the chicken fillets with salt and pepper. (If using a whole chicken breast fillet, cut into broad strips.) Place a frying pan over a medium heat, then add the butter and heat until melted and lightly browned. Add the seasoned chicken fillets and sauté for 3–4 minutes until evenly coloured and just cooked through. Remove and keep warm.

**the dressing**   When the confit oil is cool, lift out the ceps with a slotted spoon and place on a board. Measure 120ml of the confit oil and put into a small bowl with the lemon juice and tarragon leaves. Season with salt and pepper and whisk to emulsify.

**to assemble**   Using a very sharp knife, cut both the ceps and artichokes into very fine slices. Arrange overlapping slices of artichoke and cep on warmed plates. Slice the chicken fillets and place on top. Spoon over the dressing and serve at once.

# Breast of wood pigeon with beetroot vinaigrette

SERVES 4

*8 thin slices pancetta or smoked bacon*

*8 wood pigeons breasts, off the bone*

*salt and pepper*

*50g butter*

**beetroot vinaigrette**

*1 medium beetroot, about 170g*

*100ml port*

*100ml vegetable nage (page 156)*

*1 tbsp balsamic vinegar*

*50ml olive oil*

*squeeze of lemon juice*

**to finish**

*100g baby beetroot leaves, baby red chard or other small salad leaves*

*2 tbsp vinaigrette (page 157)*

**beetroot vinaigrette**　Make this first. Peel the beetroot and cut into 3mm slices, then cut these slices into 3mm cubes. Put into a small saucepan and add the port and nage to cover. Bring to a simmer and cook the beetroot for 10–15 minutes until tender. Remove the beetroot with a slotted spoon and set aside on a plate. Let the cooking liquor bubble until reduced and thickened to a light syrupy consistency. Allow to cool. Add the cooked beetroot to the cooled liquor with the balsamic vinegar and olive oil. Add a squeeze of lemon juice and check the seasoning.

**oven-crisped bacon**　Preheat the oven to 210°C (200°C fan oven) Gas 6. Lay the pancetta slices side by side on a sturdy baking sheet lined with greaseproof paper. Cover with another sheet of greaseproof paper and place another heavy baking sheet on top to keep the pancetta slices flat. Cook in the oven for 8–12 minutes until crisp, then remove and drain on kitchen paper.

**cooking the pigeon breasts**　Season the wood pigeon breasts on both sides with salt and pepper. Heat a frying pan with a metal handle (suitable for use in the oven) over a high heat, then add the butter. Place the pigeon breasts, skin-side down, in the hot pan and cook for 2 minutes until golden brown, then turn and cook for a further 1 minute to sear the flesh side. Transfer the pan to the oven and cook for 3–4 minutes for medium rare; 5–6 minutes for medium. Remove and allow to rest in a warm place for 5 minutes.

**to serve**　Gently warm the beetroot in its liquor. Dress the salad leaves with the vinaigrette. Arrange two pigeon breasts, skin-side up, on each warmed plate. Spoon the warm beetroot cubes on top and drizzle with the liquor. Arrange the salad leaves alongside and finish with the crispy pancetta slices. Serve at once.

**as a canapé**  Lay slices of the foie gras terrine on toasted slices of brioche and cut into fingers. Skewer quartered pickled artichokes (page 10) on to cocktail sticks and press one into each canapé.

# Terrine of foie gras, wood pigeon & ham hock

SERVES 8–10

**jellied ham**
*1 ham hock, soaked overnight in*
  *cold water (in the fridge)*
*1 carrot, peeled and quartered*
*1 onion, peeled and quartered*
*1 leek, white only, quartered*
*1 celery stick, trimmed and halved*
*2 garlic cloves, peeled and cracked*
*1 chicken bouillon cube*
*1–2 thyme sprigs*
*1½ sheets leaf gelatine*

**fois gras**
*1 fresh foie gras, about 500g*
*100ml port*
*30ml Cognac*
*100ml Madeira*

**pigeon breasts**
*4 wood pigeon breasts*
*salt and pepper*
*1 tsp vegetable oil*
*1 tbsp unsalted butter*

**to serve**
*cornichons*
*pear chutney (page 157), or other*
  *good, fruity chutney*

**to cook the ham hock**    Put into a large pan, cover with cold water and slowly bring to the boil, then drain off the water. Cover generously with fresh cold water, bring to the boil, skim, then add the vegetables, garlic, bouillon cube and thyme. Simmer gently, skimming frequently, for 3 hours until the ham is very tender. Leave to cool in the liquor for 30 minutes.

**marinating the foie gras**    Cut the foie gras into 2–3cm slices and place in a bowl with the port, Cognac and Madeira. Leave to marinate for 2 hours.

**preparing the jellied ham**    Lift out the warm ham, take off the bone and shred with your fingers; put into a bowl. Measure 300ml of the cooking liquid into a pan and reduce by half. Meanwhile, soften the gelatine in cold water to cover for 15 minutes. Take the reduced liquor off the heat. Squeeze the gelatine leaves to remove excess water, then add to the liquor, stirring to dissolve. Pour over the shredded ham, stir, then set aside to cool.

**cooking the pigeon breasts**    Preheat the oven to 210°C (200°C fan oven) Gas 6 and season the pigeon breasts. Heat a frying pan with a metal handle (suitable for oven use) over a high heat. Add the oil, followed by the butter. Cook the pigeon breasts, skin-side down, in the hot pan for 2–3 minutes, then turn and cook on the other side for 1 minute. Transfer the pan to the oven and cook for 2–3 minutes for medium rare. Remove and rest for 10 minutes, then slice each breast in half horizontally.

**pan-frying the foie gras**    Remove the foie gras from the marinade, pat dry with kitchen paper and season. Heat a frying pan over a medium-high heat until very hot. Add the foie gras slices to the hot, dry pan and fry for 1 minute on each side until golden. Remove, let cool, then chill briefly.

**the terrine**    Line a 20 x 7.5cm terrine mould or loaf tin with a double layer of cling film, leaving overhang. Put a quarter of the ham in the bottom of the mould, press firmly and cover with a third of the foie gras, then a third of the pigeon slices. Repeat these layers twice and finish with a layer of ham. Fold the cling film over and place a small board on top (that just fits inside). Put some weights on top to press the terrine. Chill overnight.

**to serve**    Unmould the terrine, cut into thick slices using a warm sharp knife, then peel away the cling film. Arrange a terrine slice on each plate. Sprinkle with sea salt, garnish with cornichons and serve with chutney.

# Foie gras poached in Sauternes with peas

SERVES 4

50g podded fresh peas

4 slices of foie gras, about 3cm
   thick and 70–80g each

salt and pepper

sweet wine poaching liquor

1kg chicken bones or wings,
   chopped

1 onion, peeled and roughly diced

60g celeriac, peeled and roughly
   diced

1 celery stick, trimmed and
   roughly chopped

1/2 leek, roughly chopped

50g dried mushrooms

500ml Sauternes or other similar
   dessert wine

**sweet wine poaching liquor**     Prepare this in advance. Place the chicken bones or wings in a large pan or cooking pot and cover with plenty of cold water, about 2.5 litres. Bring to the boil and skim, then simmer, skimming frequently, for 20 minutes. Add the onion, celeriac, celery, leek and dried mushrooms, and gently simmer for 1 1/2 hours, skimming as necessary. Remove from the heat and allow to cool for 30 minutes. Pass the stock through a muslin-lined sieve into a clean pan; discard the bones and vegetables. Reduce, if necessary, over a medium-high heat to 1 litre. Pour half of the wine into a wide saucepan, bring to the boil and bubble to reduce until almost syrupy. Add the rest of the wine and reduce again, by about two-thirds. Now, add the chicken stock to the sweet wine reduction and return to a simmer.

**blanching the peas**     Add the peas to a pan of boiling water and blanch for 1 minute, then drain and refresh in cold water; drain and set aside.

**foie gras**     Heat a large frying pan over a high heat until very hot. Season both sides of the foie gras slices with salt and fry them on one side only for 30 seconds or until nicely caramelised, then carefully move them into the gently simmering stock. Poach the foie gras for 3–4 minutes, adding the blanched peas 1 minute before the end.

**to serve**     Very carefully lift the foie gras slices into warmed serving bowls. Taste the poaching liquor and adjust the seasoning. Pour the liquor over the foie gras, spooning in the peas. Serve immediately.

**note**     You can use the poaching liquor as the basis for a delicious soup, without the foie gras. Try flavouring it with smoked bacon or sausage: simmer about 200g in the strained soup for 30 minutes, then infuse off the heat for a further 30 minutes. Strain to remove the meat, then add a little freshly cooked sliced sausage or diced bacon before serving.

# Open ravioli of rabbit with mustard sauce

SERVES 4

*2 back legs of rabbit, skinned*

*75g butter*

*1/2 onion, peeled and roughly chopped*

*3 garlic cloves, peeled and cracked*

*1 thyme sprig*

*2 bay leaves*

*100ml white wine*

*1 litre chicken stock (page 156)*

*2 tbsp double cream*

*1 tbsp Pommery mustard*

*16 wonton wrappers (1/2 pack) or 150g fresh pasta (page 157)*

*salt and pepper*

*20 tarragon leaves, to garnish*

**to cook the rabbit**    Preheat the oven to 150°C (140°C fan oven) Gas 2. Place a small flameproof casserole over a low heat. Add 60g butter and heat until melted, then add the onion, garlic, thyme and bay leaves. Cover and sweat gently for about 8 minutes until the onion is soft. Add the wine and reduce by two-thirds, then add the rabbit legs. Pour in the stock to cover, then put the lid on. Transfer to the oven and braise for 2½ hours, until the meat falls away from the bones easily. Leave to cool in the stock for about 30 minutes. Take out the rabbit, reserving the liquor, and strip the meat from the bones. Divide into shreds and put into a bowl.

**mustard sauce**    Strain the cooking liquor into a small pan and bubble to reduce by one-third, then stir in the cream and mustard. Add 2 tsp of this sauce to the meat to keep it moist; set aside.

**to cook the wontons or pasta**    If using pasta, cut into 10cm squares; you will need 16. Add the pasta squares or wonton wrappers to a large pan of boiling salted water and cook until al dente, about 1–1½ minutes.

**to finish**    In the meantime, whisk the remaining 15g butter into the sauce, a piece at a time. Put two-thirds of the sauce in a pan over a low heat, stir in the rabbit and heat through gently; check the seasoning. Warm the remaining sauce in another pan. Place 4 spoonfuls of the hot rabbit mixture in each warmed soup plate, spacing them well apart. Top each mound of rabbit with a wonton or pasta square. Spoon the remaining mustard sauce all over the ravioli, allowing it to run through and cover the bottom of the plates. Garnish each ravioli with a tarragon leaf and serve.

**as a main course pie**    Cook the braised rabbit, take off the bone and combine with all of the creamy mustard sauce. Blanch 100g fresh peas and a chopped wedge of Savoy cabbage in boiling water for 2 minutes, then drain and combine with the rabbit mixture. Put into a 1.2 litre pie dish. Roll out a 250g pack puff pastry and use to make a lid for the pie, brushing the rim of the dish with water to seal. Glaze with beaten egg and bake at 210°C (200°C fan oven) Gas 6 for 25–30 minutes until golden.

# Seared veal carpaccio

SERVES 6

*600g veal rump, trimmed*

*salt and pepper*

*2 tbsp vegetable oil*

*20g unsalted butter*

*1 large onion, peeled and roughly
    chopped*

*2 carrots, peeled and roughly
    chopped*

*4–5 thyme sprigs*

shallot confit

*3 shallots, peeled and finely
    chopped*

*100ml extra virgin olive oil*

warm mushroom and bean salad

*100g fine green beans*

*175g mixed wild mushrooms, such
    as trompettes des morts and
    chanterelles, cleaned*

*2 tbsp olive oil*

*1 garlic clove, peeled and cracked*

*4 tbsp vinaigrette (page 157)*

to finish

*Provolone or Parmesan cheese
    shavings*

*small salad leaves, such as
    watercress and wild rocket,
    to garnish*

**shallot confit**    Prepare this first. Put the chopped shallots into a small saucepan with a pinch of salt, then cover with the 100ml extra virgin olive oil. Place over a very low heat and allow the shallots to cook slowly in the warm oil until translucent, about 30 minutes. Leave to cool.

**cooking the veal**    Preheat the oven to 230°C (220°C fan oven) Gas 8. Season the veal with salt and pepper. Heat a large frying pan with a metal handle (suitable for use in the oven) until hot. Add the vegetable oil, then the butter and heat. Put the veal into the pan and colour for 2 minutes, then turn and colour on all sides until brown all over. Remove and set aside.  Add the chopped onion, carrots and thyme sprigs. Return the veal to the pan, placing it on top of the vegetables. Transfer to the oven and roast for 5–6 minutes for medium-rare, 7–8 minutes for medium, turning the meat halfway through cooking. Remove and leave to rest in a warm place for 10 minutes.

**warm mushroom and bean salad**    Bring a pan of salted water to the boil. Add the green beans and blanch for about 2 minutes until al dente. Drain and refresh in a bowl of iced water. Drain, cut into 2cm lengths and set aside. Slice the mushrooms. Heat a large frying pan until hot, then add the olive oil and garlic. Add the mushrooms to the pan and season immediately with salt and pepper. Cook for 1–2 minutes, gently moving the mushrooms around in the pan with a wooden spoon. Tip into a bowl, discarding the garlic.

**to finish**    Slice the rested veal as thinly as possible across the grain. Add the green beans and shallot confit to the warm mushrooms with the vinaigrette. Toss gently to mix and check the seasoning. Arrange the veal slices on large warmed serving plates, overlapping the slices slightly, and season with salt and pepper. Spoon the mushroom and bean salad on top. Scatter with Provolone or Parmesan shavings and garnish with a few small salad leaves. Serve immediately.

**as a main course**   Double the
quantities — you will need a 1.2kg piece of boned
and rolled loin of veal or rump. Cook as above,
allowing about 30–40 minutes in the oven. Rest
for 10 minutes. Meanwhile, add a splash of red
wine and a cupful of veal or chicken stock to the
pan and stir to deglaze, then strain the jus. Carve
the veal into thick slices and serve with the
French beans and sauté potatoes.

# Basics

### Chicken stock   MAKES ABOUT 2 LITRES   *1kg chicken bones or wings; 1 large onion, peeled and roughly chopped; 1 leek, roughly chopped; 2 celery sticks, roughly chopped; 3 garlic cloves, peeled and cracked; 1 bay leaf; 1 thyme sprig*

Place the chicken bones or wings in a large pan or cooking pot and cover with plenty of cold water, about 2.5 litres. Bring to the boil and skim, then simmer, skimming frequently, for 20 minutes. Add the onion, leek, celery, garlic and herbs. Simmer gently for 2 hours, skimming as necessary. Remove from the heat and allow to cool for 30 minutes. Pass the stock through a muslin-lined sieve into a bowl. Cool, then refrigerate for up to 3 days and use as required.

### Fish stock   MAKES ABOUT 1½ LITRES   *600–800g white fish bones (sole, halibut etc), gills removed; 2 tbsp olive oil; ½ fennel bulb, trimmed and roughly chopped; 1 small onion, peeled and chopped; 1 leek, white part only, cleaned and roughly chopped; 1 celery stick, roughly chopped; ¼ lemon; 2 parsley sprigs*

Rinse the fish bones under cold running water and set aside. Heat the olive oil in a large heavy-based pan, add the vegetables, then cover and sweat slowly for 10–15 minutes until soft. Add the fish bones, lemon and parsley. Pour in 2 litres cold water and bring to the boil, then skim. Lower the heat and simmer gently for 20 minutes, skimming frequently. Remove from the heat and allow to cool. Pass the stock through a muslin-lined sieve into a bowl. Refrigerate for up to 2 days and use as required.

### Vegetable nage   MAKES ABOUT 2 LITRES   *2 onions, peeled; 5 carrots, peeled; 2 celery sticks; 1 leek, white part only; 2 fennel bulbs, trimmed; ½ garlic bulb, cut crossways; 5 white peppercorns; 3 star anise; 1 tsp fennel seeds; 1–2 sprigs each of chervil, tarragon, dill and flat-leaf parsley*

Roughly chop all the vegetables and place in a large pan or stockpot with the garlic and spices. Pour in 2 litres cold water to cover. Bring to the boil over a medium heat, then cover the surface with a piece of greaseproof paper and lower the heat. Simmer gently for 20 minutes. Remove from the heat and pour everything into a bowl. Add the herbs and leave to cool, then cover with cling film and leave to infuse in the fridge overnight. The next day, strain the nage through a fine sieve into a clean bowl, discarding all the flavourings. Cover and keep in the fridge for up to 3 days until ready to use.

### Shortcrust pastry   MAKES 400g   *250g plain flour, sifted; large pinch of salt; small pinch of sugar; 140g unsalted butter, diced; 1 egg, lightly beaten; 1 tbsp milk*

Put the flour, salt and sugar into a large bowl. Add the diced butter and rub into the flour, using your fingertips until the mixture looks like fine crumbs. Add the egg and half of the milk and mix to a dough. Knead lightly until smooth, adding more of the milk if the dough is too dry. Wrap the pastry dough in cling film and rest in the fridge for at least 1 hour before using.

## Pasta dough MAKES 250g *200g '00' pasta flour; 2 medium eggs; 1 tsp olive oil*

Sift the flour into a food processor. Lightly whisk the eggs and olive oil together in a small bowl. Pour half of the egg mix into the food processor and blend for about 1 minute until the mixture resembles fine crumbs. With the motor running, slowly add the remaining egg mix through the feeder tube until you have a smooth, firm dough; you may not need to add all of the egg. Wrap the pasta dough in cling film and rest in the fridge for at least 1 hour before using. When ready to use, roll out the pasta dough, in batches, using a pasta machine. Continue to pass through the machine, narrowing the setting each time until the pasta sheets are very thin, then shape and cook as required.
**note** Do not add salt to the dough, as this only will encourage discolouration.

## Vinaigrette MAKES 200ml *50ml balsamic vinegar; 150ml extra virgin olive oil; salt and pepper; 3 garlic cloves, peeled and cracked; 1 thyme sprig; 1 rosemary sprig*

Whisk the balsamic vinegar, olive oil and seasoning together in a bowl. Add the remaining ingredients and transfer to a screw-topped jar. Leave to infuse for at least 24 hours, or up to 4–5 days in the fridge. Strain and use as required. The vinaigrette can be stored in the fridge for 2–3 weeks.
**note** To vary the flavour, replace 50ml of the olive oil with walnut oil or hazelnut oil.

## Mayonnaise MAKES 500ml *4 medium egg yolks, or 2 tbsp pasteurised egg yolk; 1½ tsp Dijon mustard; ½ tsp salt; ¼ tsp white pepper; 1½ tsp white wine vinegar; 500ml vegetable or light olive oil*

Put the egg yolks, mustard, salt, pepper and wine vinegar into a bowl and whisk together. Slowly whisk in the oil, drop by drop to begin with, then in a thin stream, to emulsify. The mayonnaise should be thick and smooth. Check the seasoning. Store in the fridge for up to 3 days.
**note** If the mayonnaise splits, try this remedy. Put 1 tbsp boiling water into a clean bowl, then slowly whisk in the split mixture – it should re-emulsify. When all the split mixture is incorporated, slowly whisk in the last of the oil.

## Pear chutney MAKES ABOUT 400g *75g soft brown sugar; 80ml white wine vinegar; 1 bay leaf; ½ tsp mustard seeds; juice of ½ orange; 1 Granny Smith apple, peeled and grated; 2 star anise; 1 tbsp sultanas; pinch of salt; 4 ripe pears*

Put all the ingredients except the pears into a pan over a medium heat. Bring to a simmer and cook for 5–7 minutes, stirring occasionally, until the mixture has a syrupy consistency. Meanwhile, peel, core and dice the pears. Add to the pan and cook over a low heat, stirring occasionally, for 10–15 minutes. Check the seasoning and allow to cool. Store in a jar in the fridge, for up to a week.

# Index

# Acknowledgements

Thank you to David Haman for trying all my recipes at home, and to my girlfriend, Julia, for eating them all! Thanks also to my staff in the kitchen: Roger, Jason, Marcus and Anna for helping me with the recipes for photography.